THE BUILDINGS OF ENGLAND
BE 4
NORTH DEVON
NIKOLAUS PEVSNER

THE BUILDINGS OF ENGLAND

North Devon

BY

NIKOLAUS PEVSNER

*

PENGUIN BOOKS

HARMONDSWORTH · MIDDLESEX

FIRST PUBLISHED 1952

The author and publishers would be grateful
to any user of this book for having any errors
or omissions pointed out to them
in as much detail
as possible

MADE AND PRINTED IN GREAT BRITAIN
FOR PENGUIN BOOKS LTD
BY WILLIAM CLOWES AND SONS LTD
LONDON AND BECCLES

CONTENTS

*

*

The map at the end of the book shows all those places, whether towns, villages, or isolated buildings, which are the subject of separate entries in the text. The index on pages 197–200 gives references to the map square in which each place thus mentioned will be found

TO LUCIE

Dockworthy 1942–1944

FOREWORD

The extensive preliminary extracting of information for this volume was done by Mrs R. Schilling. The entries on prehistory were prepared by Robin Place. In addition, Katherine Michaelson and Mary Mouat have worked on it. My own journeys through Devon would probably not have been possible and certainly not have been enjoyable if it had not been for my wife's undaunted driving. Much help has been received from Mr G. W. Copeland, Mr E. Hart, Head Verger of Exeter Cathedral, Mr E. J. Coombe, Librarian of the Devon County Library, Mr N. S. E. Pugsley, Librarian of the Exeter City Library, Mr W. G. Hoskins, Mr H. P. R. Finberg, Mr Amery Adams, Hon. Treasurer of the Devonshire Association, Mr Bruce Oliver, and Mr Alfred E. Blackwell, Librarian and Curator of the North Devon Athenaeum, Barnstaple. Many vicars and rectors have been extremely helpful; only a few have been recalcitrant or downright rude. The owners of houses, with only one exception, have been most obliging. Some have taken great trouble to provide me with information. I owe it to them to make it clear that the inclusion of a house into this volume does by no means imply that it is accessible to the public.

In addition, I have had the privilege of making full use of the photograph collection of the National Buildings Record. Moreover, by the courtesy of the Ministry of Housing and Local Government, who have a statutory duty to compile lists of buildings of architectural or historic interest, I have had access to unpublished lists and much other information collected by the Chief Investigator of the Ministry and his staff (here abridged MHLG). I have also been able to use the index of Victorian churches compiled by Mr G. S. Goodhart-Rendel (here abridged GR) and the index of Victorian stained glass compiled by Sir Thomas Kendrick (here abridged TK). I wish to express my sincere thanks to both Mr Goodhart-Rendel and Sir Thomas Kendrick and also to Mr Cecil Farthing of the National Buildings Record.

I have made a point of seeing personally everything

I*

mentioned in this book. Where very occasionally that could not be done or was overlooked, entries are put in brackets. Church Plate is the only major exception. Here I have relied on published accounts. But there must be all kinds of aspects of Devon architecture which have escaped the notice of my assistants and myself, in spite of the care we have taken. I shall be most grateful to any user of this book who will draw my attention to omissions and factual mistakes. There are bound to be many.

Winter, 1951–2

INTRODUCTION*

THE size of Devonshire is 1,661,000 acres, that is, among English counties it is smaller only than Yorkshire and Lincolnshire, and it is the largest of all those which are not administratively subdivided. Its variety of landscape is in consequence exceptional. It ranges from the sub-tropical fertility of Salcombe to the grim blizzards of Princetown on Dartmoor, from the flattish dull plains in the centre to the 'English Switzerland' of Lynton and the valleys behind which were so dear to Mid-Victorians. All that can be said about the county throughout is that it is hilly and well wooded everywhere, and that its landscape features are on a large scale, as England goes, and never niggling. Otherwise, Exmoor, the W fringes of which reach into Devon, is different from Dartmoor, a little more melodious, less forbidding in outline, and lacking the granite outcrops which are the unforgettable feature of Dartmoor. The N coast is different from the S coast, though both have their lush combes. The S has many estuaries, the N really only one, the one formed by the confluence of Torridge and Taw below Bideford and Barnstaple. The S against that has, from E to W, the Axe, the Otter, the Exe, the Teign, the Dart, the Yealm, and the combined Plym, Tavy, and Tamar. The extensive winding creeks of the S find no parallel in the N. The colour of the N rocks is grey, of the S rocks red.

* This introduction deals with the architecture of Devonshire in general, including South Devon, to which a special volume of *The Buildings of England* is devoted. The borderline between the two volumes has been drawn as follows: Starting from the E it follows the A38 road to Tiverton, with places on the road contained in the South Devon volume. It then turns S to Cadeleigh Station and from there W, with Cadeleigh, Cheriton Fitzpaine, and Copplestone in the North Devon volume. From Copplestone the line runs along the B3215 road to Okehampton and then along the A30 road to Launceston (places on the two roads under South Devon). On the whole it can no doubt be objected that this borderline runs too far S, especially near Crediton, but the South Devon volume could not possibly be overweighed any more.

Geologically also Devonshire is complex. Devonian, one of the oldest formations found in Britain, derives its name from the county. It appears as dark slates and slaty lime-stones N of the Pre-Cambrian tip to a line from Newton Abbot to Tavistock; and again in the N of the county N of a line from Barnstaple to South Molton and Bampton, includ-ing Exmoor and the remarkable rocks of Lynmouth and Ilfracombe; it also incidentally fills most of Cornwall. In the centre between the two Devonian areas is Dartmoor, a granite plateau rising to a height of over 2000 ft. Farther W granite comes through again in Cornwall in Bodmin Moor and in many smaller isolated patches reaching out as far as the Isles of Scilly and Lundy Island. N of Dartmoor and S of the Devonian of North Devon is all Culm, a belt of dark shales and often siliceous sandstones, unattractive, with heavy clays on top and poor soil. It covers the area N of a line from Exeter to Okehampton, a part of NE Cornwall, the coast and hinterland from there to Barnstaple, and then S of South Molton and Bampton.

The remaining SE of Devon has the most spectacular rocks, those of the Triassic New Red Sandstone, the red cliffs of the coast from Torquay to Seaton and the red earth to the l. and r. of the river Exe up to Tiverton and N of Crediton and with a tongue running W to a little N of Oke-hampton. Some scattered patches occur also in other parts of Devon. Younger rocks come to the fore mainly in the extreme SE, a confused area containing, for example, the Jura chalk of Beer. The oolitic stones so celebrated as a building material in England from Northamptonshire to Somerset and Dorset are absent from Devon.

Devon building materials are the reflexion of this geo-logical situation: granite in and around Dartmoor, red sandstone in and around Exeter and as far N as Cullompton, Halberton and so on, and plenty of local Devonian and Culm materials otherwise. Beer stone, a limestone at the junction of chalk with greensand, is much used for fine carving, e.g. at Exeter Cathedral; flint occurs very occasion-ally in the Axminster neighbourhood. Brick reached Devon-shire late. It became accepted as a building material of dignity only during the age of Christopher Wren (Puslinch, Stedcombe, Great Torrington) although occasional C16 instances occur (Smallacombe, near Lifton; Powderham). The Devon cottage is not timber-framed with the timbers exposed. The characteristic building material is cob, whitewashed in the N, often buff-washed in the S. The angles are rounded, the roofs thickly thatched. Chimneys often project very far outside. Picturesque villages of such cottages abound, and it is impossible to single out one or a few.

The principal architectural centres are Exeter, not because of its parish churches, but because of its Cathedral, the only cathedral of the SW from 1050 to the establishment of a bishopric of Cornwall at Truro in 1876; Plymouth and Devonport, for early C19 domestic, military, and naval architecture; and the prosperous wool-towns such as Tiverton, Cullompton, Totnes, Ashburton. There was obviously more prosperity in the S than in the N. The S of North Devon especially is dull in its buildings. On the moors also one must not expect to find spectacular architectural displays.

Dartmoor, on the other hand (like Bodmin Moor in Cornwall), is an ideal hunting ground for the prehistory fan.* The position regarding the prehistory of Devon is this. The earliest inhabitants were the Old Stone Age men who left their stone tools in Kent's Cavern, near Torquay, during the Ice Age half a million years ago. At this time, when mammoth, reindeer, and rhinoceros roamed the countryside, Britain was still joined to the Continent. This land-bridge allowed Devon, like other parts of the country, to be occupied by representatives of the two great centres of population, Africa and Asia. The earliest farmers, men of the Later Stone Age, who invaded SW Britain from Brittany about 2300 B.C., built at Hembury, near Honiton, a typical camp with causeways left at intervals across the ditch.† Their farming was mixed, with the emphasis on cattle-breeding, and they imported axes of fine-grained stone from Cornwall.

---

* Dartmoor sites will be found in these volumes gathered together under Dartmoor North and Dartmoor South; Exmoor sites, as far as they belong to Devon, under Exmoor.

† This was later reconstructed by Iron Age folk.

Their camps do not seem to have been defensive, but were probably built to keep the cattle from straying.

In the early Bronze Age, about the year 1900 B.C., a warrior trading people known from their distinctive drinking cups as the Beaker Folk landed in s Britain from Dartmoor to Sussex. They have a special significance in the story of Devon, as they may have been the first Celtic race to invade our island. They were a branch of a tall roundheaded race who, from Spain, spread over west and central Europe. Devon was first colonized from Brittany, and later further settled by bands of the Central European branch who invaded East Anglia from the Rhineland and overran the whole country from E to W. The Beaker Folk were responsible for the erection of circular religious sanctuaries, such as Stonehenge, and also for the import of metal goods from Ireland at a time when metallurgy was unknown in Britain. These great traders may have occupied some of the undatable hutcircles on Dartmoor, but otherwise their only surviving remains are their graves. They buried their dead on their side, knees drawn up to chin, in cists constructed of large slabs of stone. This was covered by a barrow of earth, and where the barrow has disappeared, a circle of stones stands out which it formerly covered. Later in the Bronze Age, when another people called the Urn Folk had replaced the Beaker Folk in Devon; Trowlesworthy and Standon Down show that these farmers lived in circular huts grouped into small communities known as hut-circles, and farmed inside irregular enclosures known as pounds. At Trowlesworthy the inhabitants of the forty huts shared 4 acres of ground; on Standon Down are fifteen plots comprising 5 acres, beside which are scattered sixty huts.

The vast majority of the prehistoric remains of Devonshire are on Dartmoor. The density of the remains proves extensive habitation of this wind-swept high-land. They can only rarely be reliably dated, but such evidence as there is points to their having been constructed during the Bronze Age. Pounds, e.g. Grimspound, enclose a number of hutcircles with a stone wall. They seem to have been farming settlements, not military camps, as they are not on defensible sites but rather on agricultural land. Water, essential to a military site, is rarely to be found nearer than 100 yards to the outer wall of the pound. The huts of the hut-circles consist of loose stone walls, some still standing to a height of nearly 4 ft, others retaining only a single course. They may have been roofed with branches and turf supported in the centre by a post the socket for which may be seen in some huts in a central stone. The hearth was either beside this stone in the middle of the floor or against the wall, and close to it was a 'cooking hole' 1 ft 3 in. deep. Across part of the floor was a dais, probably for the beds. Stone alignments, e.g. Merrivale, are of unknown date and purpose. Some of them lead away from Bronze Age barrows, and seem to be associated with a cult of the dead, but others stand alone. In many of the Dartmoor examples a single stone blocks the end of the row. Stone Circles, e.g. the Nine Stones near Okehampton, also appear to be connected with a cult of the dead. They may be either the retaining wall of a now vanished barrow or a free-standing circle erected round it, possibly with the idea of terrifying the ghosts. While the Beaker Folk buried their dead in barrows, the Urn Folk cremated theirs and buried the ashes in urns.

The Iron Age in sw Britain began about 450 B.C. Cornwall was invaded by tin-seekers from Brittany, and this militant people, with their iron tools, spread over the sw. In Devon the insecurity of the Iron Age, the period of great tribal movements on the Continent, is reflected by the construction of hill forts, e.g. Hembury and Woodbury Castle, and by the occupation of caves as refuges.

The Roman Conquest in A.D. 43 marks by no means a clear-cut end of the Iron Age. Surviving evidence in Devon and Cornwall makes it unlikely that the Romans ever completely conquered the sw. A Roman road led as far as Exeter (Isca Dumnoniorum) and not farther. A Roman pavement survives at Exeter. Three villas have been discovered, all three E of Exeter, one at Holcombe near Uffculme, close to the Dorset border, the others near Seaton. Romano-British inscribed stones are less interesting than in Cornwall. When the Saxons arrived in Devon, they seem to have found a vacuum, as it were. The Romans had gone, and the British presumably retired into Cornwall. This appears the only explanation of the marked scarcity of Celtic place-names (less than 1 per cent). Yet there is hardly any visible record of the presence of the Saxons in Devon, other than a few decorated crosses and fragments of crosses. That at Colyton is indubitably the best. Others are at Dolton (used as a font), Copplestone, and Exeter Priory. At Sidbury a stone-slab with interlace work was found some time ago. Sidbury also possesses a small and completely plain Saxon crypt. Otherwise no building or part of a building remains.

Architectural evidence becomes at once much more copious when the Norman Conquest is reached. Although there is only one major document, the transeptal towers of Exeter Cathedral, there is plenty of minor evidence. Church towers are the most usual reminder of the C12 and C13, un-dated but as a rule chronologically easily placed. Their solidity as compared with the rest of the church preserved them. It needed a good deal of pride and money to pull down a tower and replace it by one bigger and better.* Most of the Norman towers are unbuttressed. Some, especially N of Bolt Head, have corbel-tables below the battlements. The majority are placed at the W end of the church, often so slim in girth as to make the nave appear wide behind them. A number of Norman towers, however, are transeptally placed, perhaps on the pattern of Exeter, although parish churches never have, of course, two such towers. I counted three in South Devon (of which two are at Exeter) and fifteen in North Devon. In addition, about a dozen exist in Cornwall (e.g. Bodmin). Amongst the churches with transeptal towers are such important examples as Barnstaple, Braunton, and Ilfracombe. While on the subject of towers, it may be mentioned in passing that towers over the crossings of churches are extremely rare in Devon (Aveton Giffard, Axminster, Branscombe, Colyton, Crediton, Kingsbridge, Shute,

* A particularly good and complete example is Sidbury, which incidentally has a room on the ground-floor covered by the earliest rib-vault in Devon. The ribs have a plain, completely unmoulded rectangular profile.

Tawstock) as against their popularity in Wiltshire, Dorset, and other counties.

Additional early medieval evidence is often the plan or part of the plan of a church. Norman (and also E.E.) churches were apparently usually aisleless and consisted of nave, transepts, and chancel. Occasionally, as at Aveton Giffard, Brentor, Hascombe, Honeychurch, West Down, West Ogwell, the early plan is preserved complete. Much more often only one-half of it survives. This is the case where the late Middle Ages have added one aisle to the nave. Thus one frequently finds churches with an aisle along one side of the nave and a transept off the other. Not all Norman churches in Devon, however, were aisleless. Piers and arcades can occasionally be found, notably at St Mary Arches Exeter, Axmouth, Farway, Hawkchurch, Mariansleigh, Membury, North Petherwin, Salcombe Regis, Sidbury. For some reason never sufficiently explained, later centuries showed the greatest respect for Norman doorways and their tympana and for fonts. Of doorways, nearly always on the s side of the church, there are far more than can here be enumerated. A specially richly decorated example is at Bishopsteignton. Others, of almost identical design, can be seen at Buckland Brewer, Shebbear, and Woolsery; but none in Devon show as much exuberance as doorways in other counties. Tympana also do not compare favourably with those of the rest of England. Bishopsteignton is perhaps the most remarkable of them, if chiefly because of its ruthless barbarity. A little figure sculpture not attached to a doorway appears at Sidbury.

Of Norman fonts there are more than a hundred in Devon (and as many again in Cornwall). They fall clearly into a number of groups, of which only the most noteworthy can here be singled out. The most elementary shape resembles an egg-cup without any pronounced structural articulation (Bridgerule). Elementary also is the reproduction of the square Early Norman block capital as a font (undecorated, for example, at Clovelly and Instow, with decoration of the four semicircular surfaces, e.g. High Bickington) and another square type of bowl with the under-edge boldly scalloped (three scallops: Weare Giffard,

Halberton; five scallops: Netherexe; decorated bowl and scallops: Hartland). The most usual structurally articulated form is that of the goblet, i.e. a roughly semicircular bowl on a columnar or conically tapering shaft. One group of these in red sandstone is frequent S of a line from Plymouth via Ivybridge to Newton Abbot. The decoration is a palmette frieze with along the upper rim a cable moulding and towards the bottom of the bowl a zigzag; or the cable is replaced by a frieze of small crosses saltire (i.e. the type of Fowey in Cornwall), and the palmettes occasionally by a frieze of running scrolls (Farringdon), or a number of rosettes in circles (Combe-in-Teignhead) or even such motifs as incised dragons (Dean Prior). Then there are some more ambitious and rare square bowls with big, coarse, human faces at the corners and usually rosettes in circles or 'trees of life' or such motifs on the sides (the type of Altarnun, St Thomas Launceston, and many others in Cornwall). This appears, for example, at Bratton Clovelly and Ashwater. A curious variation on this theme are the fonts at Clawton and Tetcott, whose bases are like this type of square bowl in reverse. The most ferociously carved of all Devon fonts also belong to this type, those at Luppit with agitated scenes along the main surfaces between the faces, and at Stoke Canon with whole human figures along the angles crouching downwards, and caryatid figures on the shaft. In addition there are quite a number of fonts of a type familiar from other counties as well. They have square, shallow bowls, rather like heavy table tops, and along the sides plain shallow friezes of roundheaded arches. They were made of Purbeck marble at or near the Purbeck quarries in Dorset. Examples are at Clyst Honiton, Crediton, Dodbrooke, Hemyock, Hennock, Kenn, Malborough, Southleigh, Talaton, etc.*

Another important addition to the architectural scene of Devon made by the Normans, but one scarcely visible any longer, was the establishment of many new monastic houses. Dugdale's *Monasticon* counts thirty-eight religious founda-

* The type is especially frequent in Cornwall and is called, in the Cornish volume of *The Buildings of England*, the Egloshayle type.

tions in Devon, thirty-five for monks and three (Polsloe before 1160, Benedictine; Canonsleigh *c.* 1170 and Cornworthy *c.* 1205–30, Augustinian) for nuns. Amongst these the most powerful were Plympton Priory (Augustinian Canons, founded early C12) and Tavistock Abbey (Benedictines, founded *c.* 974). The only abbey in North Devon was Hartland (Augustinian, founded mid C12). Other monasteries of which more or less insignificant remains can still be seen are St Nicholas, Exeter (founded 1080) and Totnes (founded *c.* 1090), both Benedictine; Barnstaple (founded *c.* 1107), Frithelstock (founded 1220), Augustinian with the architecturally most impressive monastic remains of Devon; Buckfast (pre-Conquest, refounded 1148, rebuilt since 1882), Dunkeswell (1201), Newenham near Axminster (1245), and Buckland (1278), all Cistercian; and Tor Abbey, Torquay (1196), Premonstratensian. The only noteworthy remains of a Friars' house are those of the Dominicans at Plymouth.

This list, however, has taken us well beyond the Norman period in architecture. E.E. remains are scarce: the Exeter Cathedral Chapter House, the chapels of Bishop Branscombe at the Bishop's Palace, Exeter, and his summer residence at Clyst Honiton, and Branscombe Church itself, where the crossing tower is Norman, the transepts E.E., and the chancel late C13. With the late C13 the architectural importance of Devon begins to rise, owing chiefly to the rebuilding of Exeter Cathedral between *c.* 1275 and *c.* 1360. The design of *c.* 1275 with its palm-tree-like sprouting and spreading piers and ribs is one of the most beautiful in medieval English architecture, though at the time when the nave was carried on according to it, i.e. about 1327–60, it had become decidedly conservative. The sixteenfold subdivided piers of Exeter and the equally spliced-up arch mouldings were (with the one exception of Cheriton Fitzpaine) never imitated in Devon. Parish churches of the late C13 and early C14 are very restrained in character. Exeter tracery also takes to flowing forms only after *c.* 1330, and even then reluctantly.* In parish churches the vagaries of

* The E window of Plympton St Mary is influenced by Exeter

Dec tracery are nowhere popular (cf., however, the stars in
the tracery of Ipplepen, Littlehempston, Plympton, Sherford, and Staverton). Even so restrained a form of undulating
tracery as the motif of ogee reticulation is rare (Clayhanger,
Dittisham, Farway, Milton Damerel, Mortehoe, Tawstock,
West Down). As a church essentially preserved in its early
C14 form Haccombe (consecrated 1328) deserves notice.
Other good examples are Bere Ferrers and Tawstock. A
much more ambitious C14 building remaining virtually in
its original state is the collegiate church of Ottery St Mary.
The college was established by Bishop Grandisson in 1337,
and the church was built quickly. Its most interesting
features are its elaborate vaults, partly with curved ribs,
in style decisively in advance of Exeter. The best things at
Ottery are the stone furnishings, such as the reredos, the
parclose screens (the earliest in Devon) and the Grandisson
monuments, though none of them can vie with the splen-
dours of the Dec style at Exeter, both in stone (rood screen,
sedilia, several monuments) and in wood (Bishop's throne).
Monuments with architectural decoration in parish churches
are at Bere Ferrers and Mortehoe, effigies without canopies
or suchlike enrichments in several places, e.g. Landkey,
Weare Giffard, Kingskerswell.

The Perp style marks the Golden Age of Devon church
architecture. It can safely be said that 95 per cent of the
work visible in the pre-Victorian churches of Devonshire
dates from between 1360 and 1530 and mostly 1400 and
1530. It is impressive in bulk, impressive in occasional
architectural details, impressive often in its furnishings, but
turns out to be singularly, distressingly, standardized, when
it is studied and recorded in detail. The elements are far too
easily enumerated.

Towers are, with few exceptions, at the w end, and belong
with few exceptions to one of two types. Type A has the
buttresses projecting diagonally from the angles, type B at
right angles from the walls and a little set back from the
angles so that these remain visible (see the illustrations
which appear in the glossary on p. 175). Real angle-buttresses,
i.e. buttresses projecting L-wise at right angles direct from

the corner, are rare. A few of the big Devon towers have type A buttresses (Bideford, Chawleigh, Highweek, Moretonhampstead, Northam, Weare Giffard, etc.), but the majority of the towers put up with the intention to impress by a display of wealth is of type B. A choice of the most remarkable is hard. Chittlehampton (115 ft high), South Molton (107 ft), Hartland (130 ft), Chulmleigh, Holsworthy, Combe Martin in North Devon, and Ashburton, Plymouth, Tavistock, Totnes in South Devon would be amongst them. They are all late Perp – Cullompton was begun as late as 1549 – and most of them show a marked Somerset influence in such motifs as large bell-openings or pinnacles on the set-offs of buttresses. Characteristic Devon towers are sheerer and more austere. The most impressive group is perhaps the one with a polygonal stair-turret placed centrally against the main show-side, usually the s side, of the tower. To this group belong Ashburton (before 1449), Totnes (shortly after 1449), Kingsteignton, Littlehempston, Harberton, Torbryan, and Ipplepen. Pinnacles on the battlements are frequent but not universal. w and nw of Dartmoor pinnacles are specially large, octagonal, and thickly crocketed (e.g. Plymouth St Andrew, Widecombe-in-the-Moor). Spires are the exception in Devon, although fire has deprived churches of former spires in a good many cases (e.g. South Molton). One clearly defined group is around Kingsbridge reaching as far w as Holbeton and as far n as Diptford and Buckfastleigh. Modbury (c13) is the earliest of them. Another group has its centre at Barnstaple and includes Braunton, Ashford, Swimbridge, and Bishops Tawton.

When the c15 and c16 enlarged existing churches, the most usual thing was to add an aisle or aisles, thus widening the area available to the congregation. Chancels rarely needed extensions. Nearly all Devon churches are what the historians of architecture call hall-churches, i.e. churches in which the aisles are of the same height as the nave. There are no more than ten churches with clerestories, i.e. naves with their own upper windows, in Devon. They are Exeter Cathedral, Crediton, Ottery St Mary, Tiverton, Cullompton, and Culmstock in South Devon, South and North Molton, Pyworthy, and North Petherwin in North Devon. North Petherwin has the windows above the arcade piers instead of the apexes of the arcade arches, an anomaly typical of Cornwall (St Germans, Lostwithiel, Fowey, Callington). Where two aisles were built, they were often carried right through to the E end of the chancel in the form of chancel chapels, mostly appropriated as chantry chapels by influential families. Where such chapels exist to the N and S of the chancel, a fine E view of the church results, with three parallel gables and three large windows. The old transepts of C12 and C13 sometimes were made part of the new plan by keeping some of their masonry. In the largest churches, however, the Perp builders added new short transepts outside their new aisles. At Combe Martin that has resulted in a very remarkable N show-front with the transept exactly in the centre and symmetrically arranged N porch farther W and vestry farther E. The whole is embattled, the most usual decorative motif, where a little more money could be expended than usual. If more money still was available, we find ornamentation (also of towers) with quatrefoil friezes and openwork battlements. The most sumptuous displays of Perp architecture in Devon are the Greenway Aisle at Tiverton with an ornamental depressed tunnel vault, the fan-vaulted Lane Aisle at Cullompton (very noble in proportions), and the Dorset Aisle at Ottery St Mary, also fan-vaulted. Smaller fan-vaults occur in the porches of Holcombe Rogus and Torbryan, a tierceron-vault at Berry Pomeroy, lierne-vaults at Brixham and Plympton.

Naves and aisles are nowhere vaulted (except at Exeter and Ottery). Their almost universal covering is the timber-roof known as the wagon-roof or cradle-roof. Its distinguishing feature is the existence of curved braces to every rafter. The effect is indeed like that of the canvas of a wagon, especially if the spaces between the timbers are plastered or ceiled. It has never yet been established whether this plastering was a medieval habit at all or only introduced later. Most of the Devon wagon-roofs have decorated bosses at the main intersections. A few emphasize the bays above the rood screen felicitously by a 'ceilure', i.e. a boarding and cross-ribbing of the panels between the main timbers and in addition their adornment by suns, stars or suchlike motifs (Hatherleigh, Hennock, Ideford, Ilfracombe, Kingsnympton, Lapford, Swimbridge, etc.). At Cullompton, Chawleigh, and Payhembury the whole roof is treated in this splendid way, at Beaford and Ugborough a whole aisle, at Hartland a whole chancel chapel. Where the chancel is not lower (i.e. usually older) and its entry stressed by a chancel arch, these wagon-roofs run uninterrupted from W to E. Emphasis on the crossing is lacking except in the three churches of Honiton (renewed), Ilsington, and Luppit, where in a remarkably original way the joiners have created the impression of a crossing by throwing semicircular braces diagonally across the space at the E end of the nave. The result is a huge open cross-rib vault of timber. At Ilsington the effect is particularly intricate.

Perp arcades between nave and aisle are disappointing. Here again, and even more than with the towers, is a case of crushing uniformity. With the exception of about two dozen examples all Perp piers in Devon belong to one of three types: A has four shafts in the main directions and four hollows in the diagonals. B has the same four main shafts, but a wavy line instead of the concave quarter-circle in the diagonals. C is simply octagonal. Octagonal piers go back in England as far as the C12 (Peterborough, Canterbury Cathedral choir). In Devon they certainly existed before A and B, although not every octagonal pier can be regarded as older than every A or B pier. The choice between the types was largely one of available materials. Octagonal piers exist in the red sandstone as well as the granite areas. Masons who had to work in granite could also cope with A, but not with B. So A is the standard form in the granite districts, B in the others. A exists, however, in two varieties according to the size of the diagonal hollow. With wide, broad hollows carried right up into the arches (without intervening capitals) it is frequent in Somerset, Dorset, Wiltshire as well; with a narrow

A-type

B-type

hollow it is typical of Devon and Cornwall 'granite. In this book no distinction is made between the two; they are both called A. Capitals of A and B are either confined to the shafts so that, as was said just now, the diagonal mouldings run uninterruptedly up into the arches, or are bands or strips, sometimes moulded but usually decorated with a horizontal frieze of large leaves. These leaf-frieze capitals will be called in this book Devon standard capitals.

Perp windows and their tracery are relatively uniform too, though not so standardized as piers. Tracery often does not lend itself to brief description and is therefore rather neglected in these pages. Two showpieces are the w windows of Colyton and of the Dorset Aisle at Ottery St Mary. Taking the whole evidence of the county, it can be said that sharply pointed arches are earlier than depressed or low four-centred arches and that straightheaded windows are later still. But a chronology of Perp tracery has yet to be established, and this could be done only on a national scale.

Another question not yet answered is at what time the Devon parish church type was complete. How far back do these piers, arches and roofs go? All that I would venture to say is that, if the suggested dates of 1377 for Brixham and 1372 for Dartmouth are accepted, then B type piers with four capitals as well as standard strip-capitals were in use then, i.e. from the very beginning of the Perp style.

Now to the furnishings of the Perp churches. Naturally, Devonshire ROOD SCREENS take the first place. They are rightly famed, and, when first seen in good and complete examples, indeed dazzling. Originally every church seems to have possessed one, and there are, including fragmentary survivals, well over a hundred left to this day. The earliest and the most sumptuous screens are of stone, especially those of Exeter and Ottery St Mary, but in parish churches nearly all of them are of timber.* Most, if not all, originally carried a loft with a parapet to the w and the E, whether that

* Excellent later exceptions Totnes (the design like Exeter Lady Chapel), Awliscombe, Colyton, Culmstock, Dunsford. Such stone screens are often combined with chantry chapels and monuments, for example at Bideford and Marldon.

parapet was supported by a coving or not. Only at Atherington does a complete rood loft remain (and at Marwood the E
parapet).* Some screens only separate the chancel from the
nave, but others include both aisles and run all the way
through from N to S. If they cross the arcade just where the
piers stand (which is the most reasonable thing to do), then
some provision had to be made for that encounter. At Swimbridge are openings left for a small altar to be placed against
the pier and forward-curving panels above it serve as a
reredos. At Bradninch, Broadhempston, Dunchideock,
Harberton, Kenn, and Torbryan the piers are encased by the
screen. Rood screens consist of the wainscoting, decorated
with tracery or – often in South Devon, hardly ever in North
Devon – painted figures of Saints, etc. With the exception
of Ashton, an early example, the standard of these paintings is deplorable. Then follows the screen proper, either –
in the simplest and probably earliest cases (Parracombe,
Tawstock) – consisting of narrowly set mullions separating
single lights which end in arches, and a straight cornice on
top, or with mullions grouped window-wise into four lights

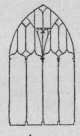

A-type

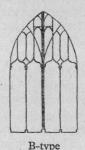

B-type

with conventional top tracery. The vast majority of the
Devon screens is treated like that, and their tracery can be
divided into two types: A with the main pointed arch subdivided into the pointed sub-arches belonging each to two
lights below and a spheric quadrangle as a spandrel between
the sub-arches and filling the space to the apex of the main

* Well reconstructed rood loft at Kenton.

arch, and B with the central mullion of the four lights thicker than the others and carried right up to the apex of the main arch, thus completely separating the two sub-arches from each other.

Outstandingly impressive examples of A are, for example, at Bovey Tracey, Bradninch, Buckland-in-the-Moor, Chawleigh, Chumleigh, Coleridge, Down St Mary, Dunchideock, Feniton, Harberton, Ipplepen, Kenn, Kentisbeare, Kenton, Kingsnympton, Manaton, Marwood, Paignton, Pinhoe, Plymtree, Staverton, Talaton, Uffculme; of B at Atherington, Broadhempston, Burrington, Halberton, Hartland, Lapford, Payhembury, Plympton St Maurice, and Swimbridge. B is decidedly rarer than A. The approximate date when these two types first appeared cannot be established. Of type A Bovey Tracey, of type B Halberton and Uffculme are ascribed in the literature to the first third of the C15, but apparently without sufficient documentary proof. One of the greatest delights of Devon screens is their ribbed coving above the arches, and above this, covering the cornice, friezes of densely carved foliage, sometimes with little figures of birds or men sitting or crawling in it. In the decoration of the screens the transition from Perp to Early Renaissance, i.e. Italian, motifs can be studied with profit. Dates are unfortunately scanty. It is, however, revealing that East Allington is dated 1547 and shows no Renaissance details whatever. Holbeton and Lustleigh with their playful Italian motifs are supposed to belong to the end of the 40s and the 50s. Other screens with Renaissance ornament are at Atherington, Lapford, and Morchard Bishop.

In addition to the standard types of screens three special local types of limited application must be mentioned. One is confined to Dartmouth and the country w of the town (St Saviour Dartmouth, Chivelstone, Portlemouth, Rattery Sherford, South Pool). It differs from the A standard only in the tracery design. The four lights of each division have semicircular heads and two are tied together by crocketed ogee gables. A second local variety of great charm is to be found at Holbeton and Ugborough.* The four lights of each

* Stoke-in-Teignhead may be an earlier and bolder form of it.

division are again roundheaded, but above them are interlaced ogee arches and in the spandrels charming openwork
leaf, tendril and scroll motifs. Finally there are Coldridge,
Colebrook and Brushford, all close together and all N of
Crediton and North Tawton. They are distinguished by
highly fanciful Flamboyant tracery under French or Spanish influence. Both the last types are straightheaded and
appear never to have had coving.

Compared with Devon screens Devon PULPITS of the
Perp style are oddly coarse, if equally exuberant in decoration. The noteworthy ones are nearly all of stone. Only
Pilton is of a type common to all England. The others have
as a rule in the main panels small badly carved figures under
nodding ogee canopies or triangularly projecting canopies
and either thickly foliated buttresses (Chittlehampton,
Swimbridge, etc.) or even more thickly foliated frames
(Dartmouth, Dartington, Dittisham, Harberton, Torbryan,
etc.) between them. They are all grossly encrusted with this
leaf decoration, whereas tracery plays only a minor part in
their design.

Perp FONTS are dull on the whole, mostly octagonal and
very often with quatrefoil decoration (e.g. Chittlehampton,
Kingsteignton, Woodbury). Carved BENCH-ENDS are frequent (more in N than S Devon) and of the same type as the
more famous series in Cornwall, i.e. the ends are rectangular
without sloping or pointed tops and without poppy-heads.*
The decoration is in South Devon usually just blank
tracery in two tiers, in North Devon initials (mostly
unexplained), shields with or without coats of arms, and also
figures of saints, the folk-art symbols of the Passion (ladder,
nails, sponge, tongs, etc.; also occasionally such odd sub-
jects as Malchus's ear) and much tracery and foliage. In the
latter the arrival of the Italian fashion can be watched. It
came late. Hartland of 1530 and North Lew of 1537 have no
Renaissance motifs; Dowland of 1546 has. The type is still
unchanged at Braunton, where dates between 1560 and
1593 are recorded, and at Alwington, where the date 1580
appears. The Renaissance brings a typical new foliage, heads

* Poppy-heads occur only at Ilsington.

in roundels, and other equally familiar motifs. Altogether it
can be assumed that the sudden introduction of benches,
obviously made by the same workmen or workshops, in so
many churches of the SW has something to do with the
Reformation and the growing importance of the sermon in
church services. The largest assemblies of carved bench-
ends in Devon are at East Budleigh and High Bickington.
A Coldridge bench-end is specially interesting for its inscription commemorating the date 1511 and the donor of
much of the church furnishings, Sir John Evans. Bench
backs and fronts are also occasionally preserved (Braunton,
Frithelstock, etc.).

Barnstaple seems to have manufactured TILES with such
patterns as fleur-de-lis, rose, lion, pelican, etc. They survive
in more than two dozen places, particularly in North Devon
(and also at Launcells in Cornwall). Medieval STAINED
GLASS is rare: the best is to be found along the Teign
Valley, with Doddiscombsleigh an easy first. North Devon
has hardly any worth tarrying over. Old VESTMENTS also
are far from frequent (Brixham, Culmstock, Holcombe
Burnell, Exeter St Petrock, Malborough, Woodland).
Church BELLS are not included in these volumes. Among
church PLATE pre-Reformation items are almost absent.
The exceptions are the chalice from Bishop Bitton's tomb at
Exeter Cathedral, two mazers in Exeter parish churches, a
paten at Brushford (C15), and chalices at Ashprington (C13),
Littleham (C14), West Hill, and Combe Pyne (both early
C16). A highly singular item is the PYX at Warkleigh, a
wooden box to protect the Holy Sacrament probably while
carried to the sick.

Late medieval SCULPTURE, where it occurs, is nearly
always of poor quality. If Perp chantry chapels, easter
sepulchres, and monuments in recesses are impressive, it is
due to their decorative rather than their sculptural qualities.
In detail there is here a great deal of variety; nothing like the
standardization of piers or screens. Of many examples the
following, in addition, of course, to the great number in
Exeter Cathedral (Sylke, Speke, Oldham Chantries, etc.),
may be singled out: Ashwater, 1442?; Bideford, 1513;

Bondleigh, Colyton, 1449; Heanton Punchardon, 1523; Holcombe Burnell; South Pool; Woodleigh; and the gloriously ornate, utterly unrestrained Kirkham Chantry at Paignton. Devon is not a county of BRASSES. The earliest with effigy is at Stoke-in-Teignhead (*c.* 1375). Easily the best are that to J. Hanley and wives at Dartmouth, 1408, and that to Sir Peter Courtenay at Exeter Cathedral, 1409.

It is these families of the old nobility and the new wealth who built the medieval CASTLES and MANOR HOUSES of Devon. In them we find as much variety and surprise of plan and detail as we find standardization in church architecture. They are thus in more than one way more rewarding to the student than the churches. For the C12 and C13 one has to go to Rougemont Castle, Exeter, and to the Keeps of Gidleigh, Lydford, and Okehampton. The most impressive later medieval castles are no doubt Tiverton (with its C14 detail) and Powderham (under the cloak of all its later re-adjustments and additions). The late C14 plan and hall of Dartington are of far more than regional interest. So are the early C16 fortified front of Compton Castle and the bay-windowed C15 to C16 front of Bradley, near Newton Abbot. The choice of other manor houses for inclusion in this summary is odious; there is so much to enjoy and study. On a large scale Holcombe Court and Weare Giffard may rank first, on a small scale Littlehempston, Wortham, and perhaps Morwell. Two of the rare town houses of before the Reformation exist in Devon, one at Plymouth (Prysten House) and one at North Tawton. Interior features of great interest are the C13 oak screen at Polsloe, near Exeter, and the pinnacled C15 screen at Wortham. The most impressive roof is at Weare Giffard (hammerbeam). Other roofs are at Cadhay, Slade, near Cornwood, Bradley, near Newton Abbot, and Orleigh. Panelling survives in many places, especially much, though badly tampered with, at Weare Giffard. It shows how, probably about 1535 or 1540, Early Renaissance ornament replaced the linenfold patterns of the Perp style.

The Renaissance, it has been said before, came late to the sw. Devon was a conservative corner – as witnessed by the

tenacious adherence to Roman Catholicism (Rising of 1549).
Perp forms are still carried on as late as the Waldron monument and almshouses at Tiverton, i.e. to *c.* 1580, the Haydon
tomb at Ottery of 1587, and later still at the Charles Church,
Plymouth, of 1640–58, Great Torrington Church in 1651,
and St Thomas, Exeter, of 1664, and even – in very secluded
corners – the schools at Plympton of 1664, Kingsbridge of
1670 and Buckland Monachorum of 1702, and the chapel
at South Zeal of 1713. It will be seen later that Jacobean
ornamentation died equally hard in the C17. Meanwhile the
Elizabethan style with its characteristic E- and H-shaped
plans, its large, straight, mullioned and transomed, tracery-
less windows, and its overelaborate woodwork and plasterwork arrived about 1560 or 1570. The transition from Early
to Late Tudor can best be seen at Cadhay. Of Elizabethan
and Jacobean houses Devon possesses none on as grand a
scale as, say, Hardwick or Wollaton or Hatfield. The most
ambitious are Borringdon, Bowringsleigh, Bradfield, Ford
near Newton Abbot, and Sydenham. Picturesque town
houses with overhanging upper storeys and quaint woodwork
survive chiefly at Dartmouth and Plymouth. Of urban
architecture the quaintest example, however, is the Exeter
Guildhall, amazingly robust and uncivilized. Mention may
also be made of the Butter Walk at Totnes and the almshouses of Moretonhampstead and Barnstaple. Plaster
decoration of high skill can in addition be admired at Barnstaple (Red Lion), Rashleigh Barton, and Holcombe Court
in North Devon, and at The Grange, Broadhembury in
South Devon. For woodwork one may go to Bradninch and
also to Great Fulford and Sydenham.

Elizabethan and Jacobean CHURCH DECORATION must
always have been more modest than the work done by the
same patrons in their houses, and it is characteristic that the
elaborate Pew at Alwington was transferred from the Hall at
Portledge. Of other family pews the most interesting, because of its relatively early date, *c.* 1540–50, is no doubt at
Tawstock. The Bluett Pew at Holcombe Rogus is early C17.
'Jacobean' screens are at Clayhanger, Colyton, Rose Ash
(1618), and Westfield (1624), 'Jacobean' pulpits in many

places. Their dating is far from easy. They may in fact go
back to the later c16, but they also survive in a virtually
unchanged style to Clovelly (1634), Horwood (1635), and
Tackbere (1693). Specially rich is the pulpit at Shebbear,
with three tiers of barbaric little figures in blank arcades.
The w Gallery at Sandford is as late as 1657 and yet still
Jacobean in character. So is the chancel panelling at Braunton of 1653. Particularly handsome chancel panelling is at
North Molton. A rarity is the c17 plaster vault at Exminster.
The most frequent items among Devon church PLATE by
far are chalices and patens made in the 1570s by Exeter
(*Jons*) and Barnstaple (*Coton, Mathew*) silversmiths.* The
differences between the two towns are marked but minor.

In church MONUMENTS of 1550–1650 Devon is neither
as rich as the Home Counties nor on the whole as good.
There is really nothing of the very first quality anywhere,
and some of the biggest monuments are of baffling rawness
(Berry Pomeroy, Holbeton). The largest type, standing,
with columns and vault, is represented at Cadeleigh (1637),
Colyton (1635), Marystow (1629), Tawstock (1589), Wembury (1608). There are several reduced versions of this type,
e.g. with pilasters instead of columns and an arch instead of
a vault (Torquay, Crediton, etc.). Other types are, of course,
the most usual minor one of Britain, with kneeling figures
opposite each other and separated by a prayer-desk, and –
more interesting – with one seated figure with head propped
up by the arm and cheek in hand (Crediton, Kenton, Plymouth, Newton St Cyres, all round about 1630), with
frontal demi-figures in niches or oval medallions (often in n
Devon, e.g. Alwington, Barnstaple, Combe Martin specially
good, East Down, Monkleigh, Swimbridge, West Down:
the first of these is 1617, the others between 1630 and 1665),
and with standing figures. The latter are specially important as starting one of the principal types for the c18.
They are to be seen at Ottery St Mary (1652), Newton St
Cyres (1632) and Eggesford (1630). At Tamerton Foliot a
monument with an upright figure in a shroud exists. It is

* Not patens, strictly speaking, but in these pages not distinguished
from them.

supposed to date from 1617, but must be later, as it is
designed on the pattern of John Donne's monument in St
Paul's Cathedral, London.

Sculpture in the new grand manner, on French or Italian
Baroque examples, is very rare (Fifth Earl of Bath,
Tawstock, c. 1680, Lady Narborough, Wembury, 1678). A
typological exception is the standing statue of Lady Fane by
Burman at Tawstock (1680). Big epitaphs with columns,
pediments and leaf scrolls or garlands in the Wren-Gibbons
style are frequent. At Clovelly, for example, they can be
followed from c. 1650 to about 1730. An interesting early
c18 Devon sculptor is *Weston* (Exeter St Martin, Ashspring-
ton, Whitchurch).

The corresponding style in architecture is poorly represented. Obviously Devon did not build much after the
Restoration and into the c18. Brick now became an accepted
material for town and country houses. Of town houses
interesting c17 and c18 examples under obvious Dutch influence remain at Topsham, and two much grander ones at
Great Torrington. Slate-hanging occurs from Topsham w
into Cornwall. The best brick country houses are Plympton
and Puslinch, of the same type as Cruwys Morchard and
Dunsland are in stone. Dunsland has inside plasterwork and
woodwork of the late c17 which is of the very highest skill
to be found anywhere in England at the time. The same
craftsmen must have worked at Bideford. The exquisitely
carved contemporary staircase at Cross, however, is not
Devon production. It came from Stow in Cornwall. Also
ornate, but much more robust, are the Gateway to the
Plymouth Citadel (1670) and the provincial (and therefore
particularly jolly) Exchange at Barnstaple of 1708, known as
Queen Anne's Walk. Otherwise public buildings of the c18
are of minor size and importance (Barnstaple, Great Torrington, South Molton) with one exception, the buildings of
the Naval Dockyard and Naval Victualling Yard at Devonport (Plymouth), ranging in date from 1718 to the 1830s.
They are amongst the country's foremost examples of early
functionalism, powerful and convincing in an undated way.
The most impressive Georgian country houses of Devon are

Saltram, both in its original mid C18 and its splendid later rooms by *Robert Adam*, Werrington Park in the *Kent* style, Castle Hill, and some mid C18 interiors at Powderham. In the grounds of such houses small buildings were erected for decoration's or punctuation's sake, and a good number of such can still be seen: 'eye-catchers' at Werrington, Castle Hill, Upcott, medievalizing folly towers at Powderham and Haldon (Dunchideock), and so on.

C18 churchwork is scattered and of no consistent style, starting from the fine screen at Cruwys Morchard, which may well be a little earlier than 1700, and going to Werrington Church, a very early Gothic Revival oddity (1743) worthy of being better known than it is. Of the same early moment also the Gothic surround of Sir Henry Cheere's monument at Shute (1741). In village churches of the C18 the chancel was often separated from the nave not only by a screen but also by a so-called tympanum, i.e. a solid wall above the screen to fill in the chancel arch. It was used to display the Creed, the Commandments, and the Lord's Prayer. Three of these are still in existence in Devon (Mollond, Satterleigh, Trentishoe). As regards funeral monuments in churches the most distinguished names of makers from London and the Provinces occur occasionally, though Devon is certainly not rich in C18 sculpture. Impressive monuments are at Dunchideock, Georgeham, Stowford, Tawstock. Work by *Flaxman* at Buckland Filleigh, Dawlish, and Kingsbridge, by *Bacon* at Widworthy, Buckland Monachorum, Buckwell, and Ottery. At Holbeton, Plympton, and Teigngrace are monuments made by *Coade & Seely* of London in artificial stone (1801–5). Such monuments or rather their parts could be ordered from catalogues.

So here the C19 is on the doorstep, with its new materials and quantity production by casting, moulding, rolling, and similar processes.* The parallel in architecture to this new approach to decoration or applied art is the imitation of styles of the past, also repetition instead of originality. It

* The innumerable slate headstones in Devon churchyards are, of course, also quantity produced, but they are the work of craftsmen and never, therefore, are two of them exactly identical.

begins with the Gothic Revival, of which pre-1800 examples are at Clovelly Court, Haine, Hartland Abbey, Tawstock Court amongst secular, and Teigngrace Church (besides Werrington, *see* above) amongst ecclesiastical buildings. Early C19 nonconformist chapels are mostly in a minimum Gothic. There are none of special aesthetic merit, and they will therefore not be mentioned in this volume. Picturesque early C19 castellated mansions are represented by Luscombe (by *John Nash*) and additions at Powderham, the glorified old English cottage (on an absurdly large scale) by Endsleigh Cottage (by *Wyatville*). Severe neo-Grecian is best represented by *Foulston*'s Plymouth Athenaeum; other more remote styles also appear occasionally, e.g. Egyptian in one of *Foulston*'s buildings at Devonport. But *Foulston*'s great importance lies in the field of planned street architecture. It is these early C19 streets which give its character to Plymouth, Stonehouse, and Devonport, and also to much at Exeter (where, indeed, Georgian terraces, circuses, and crescents begin in the later C18), Barnstaple, etc. The seaside resorts of Devon became popular at just that time, and consequently fine terraces and crescents are to be seen at Torquay, Teignmouth, and (later) Ilfracombe. Sidmouth, on the other hand, is perhaps unparalleled for *cottages ornés*. Lynton and Lynmouth are on the whole later, Early Victorian rather than Late Georgian. This also applies to the three biggest medievalizing C19 mansions on the N coast, Watermouth, Glenthorne, and Lee Abbey. While in these mansions the C19 means battlements and bay-windows, and in villas and hotels pitched roofs and barge-boarding, in urban architecture it means Italianate instead of Neo-Classical. The transition can be observed at Plymouth, Exeter, Teignmouth, etc.

Some of the leading Victorian architects are represented in Devon buildings, e.g. *Pugin* at Bicton, *Butterfield* at St Mary Babbacombe (Torquay), and Yealmpton, *Burges* at Knighthayes, near Tiverton, *Street* at St John Torquay, *Pearson* at Landscove and All Saints Torquay, *Sir Ernest George* at Rousdon and Stoodleigh. Decoration by *Morris & Co.* can be seen at Monkton and *Morris* glass in various

other places (e.g. Emmanuel Church, Plymouth). *Sedding's*
St Peter Sheldon, *Caroë's* St David Exeter, and *Nicholson
& Corlette's* St Matthew Chalston Torquay, and St Paul
Yelverton, lead on from the period imitation of the C19 to
the originality of the C20. The international style of the mid
C20 finally appears in the houses by *Howe & Lescaze* at
Dartington.

Broadly, this is the development of architecture in Devonshire. More than such a broad survey can as yet not be given.
The detailed remarks on the following pages will often be
found inadequate or faulty. The present state of research
does not really justify an architectural guidebook such as
this. The best source of information is the *Transactions of
the Devonshire Association* (*TDA*). The best books and
articles on individual topics are: for prehistory the first
Devon volume of the *Victoria County History*, and J. and C.
Hawkes's *Prehistoric Britain*, London, 1947, with its Devon
appendix; for church architecture of the Middle Ages J.
Stabb's *Devon Church Antiquities*, London, 1909, and *Some
Old Devon Churches*, 3 vols., London, 1909–16, A. T.
Hussell's *North Devon Churches*, 1909, and much more suc-
cinctly A. Hamilton Thompson in *Archaeological Journal*,
vol. 70, 1913, B. Cresswell in *Trans. Exeter Dioc. Arch. Soc.*,
3rd Series, vol. 3, 1920, and C. Fryer Cornelius in *TDA*,
vol. 78, 1946; for towers G. W. Copeland in *An. Rep. &
Trans.* of the Plymouth Institution, vol. 17, 1935; for fonts
TDA, vols. 45–54; for screens F. Blyth Bond & B. Camm's
Roodscreens and Roodlofts, vol. 2, 1909; for bench-ends
K. M. Clarke in *Trans. Exeter Dioc. Arch. Soc.*, 3rd Series,
vol. 3, 1920; for church plate *TDA*, vols. 37–59; for man-
ions and manor houses the volumes of *Country Life* (*see* its
cumulative index published every year), and *Devonshire
Studies* by W. G. Hoskins and H. P. R. Finberg, 1952; for
gatehouses and porches G. W. Copeland in *An. Rep. &
Trans.* of the Plymouth Institution, vol. 18, 1936; for
bridges C. Henderson & E. Jervoise's *Old Devon Bridges*,
1938.

NORTH DEVON

*

ABBOTS BICKINGTON

ST JAMES. Very small and quite on its own. Prettily over-grown with ivy – a rarity nowadays, and yet it would, in the case of many small churches, be a welcome addition to their charm. Early aisleless plan with S transept (un-moulded pointed arch to the nave), and early W tower without buttresses or W door, and with minute round-headed bell-openings to N and S. The small N windows of nave and chancel pointed trefoiled, i.e. *c.* 1300. The S transept and S nave windows of two lights with tracery of about the same date. – FONT. Norman, circular, with only a little cable decoration; very damaged. – STAINED GLASS. C14–C15 fragments in the E window, a St Christopher, a Christ crucified, a St Anthony, etc. – TILES. Quite a number of the Barnstaple tiles much used in this part of Devon. – PLATE. Chalice, Paten, Flagon, and Almsdish, all 1734, by *Vincent* of London, all given by H. Rolle. – MONUMENT. Minor epitaph to Thomas Pollard † 1710, placed diagonally in the NE corner of the church.

ABBOTSHAM

ST HELEN. Quite unusual in that the broad, short tower (buttresses only at the foot, no pinnacles) is placed at the NE end. Thus a group of tower, low chancel and higher nave – the church has no aisles – is formed which is very refreshing. The plan of nave, S transept and chancel points to the C13; *see* the two lancet windows in the nave. The other windows look renewed. Inside, one is attracted by an equally exceptional feature: two completely domestic-looking two-light windows of the late C16 or C17 in the upper E wall of the nave, above the chancel arch. Original ceiled wagon-roofs in nave, transept, and chancel. – FONT. Circular, Norman, fluted bowl, cable-moulding round waist (cf. Beaford, Bradworthy, Clayhanger, and Parkham nearby). – BENCH-ENDS. Of the usual type, with representations of the Crucifixion, Christ carrying the Cross, Saints, a kneeling figure, and a tumbler, apart from the usual tracery, Perp leaves and Renaissance medallions. – PLATE. Elizabethan Chalice of Barnstaple type (by *Coton*?); Paten, 1720; Flagon, 1736. – MONUMENT. John Willett † 1736, still the late C17 type so amply represented at Clovelly.

ACLAND BARTON
1 m. N of Landkey

The original house of the Acland family. In spite of rough handling, unusually much is here preserved of a small Early Tudor manor house. The house itself has wooden doorways into the screens' passage and out of it at the back, also doors from the screens' passage to the offices, and on the upper floor (a ceiling was put in later) signs of a preserved open timber-roof with moulded beams. At right angles the chapel wing, two-storeyed, with Tudor windows and a wagon-roof with bosses. Dr Hoskins dates the house c. 1475. Alterations to the main block 1591.

AFFETON BARTON
1 m. W of West Worlington

Of the large manor house of the Stucley family the GATE-HOUSE remains upright, though much altered in 1868. The main gateway with depressed arches is filled in, but the three-storey C15 tower N of its E exit remains. Of the other buildings, e.g. the chapel, only walls survive.

ALVERDISCOTT

ALL SAINTS. Unbuttressed W tower with small pinnacles. N aisle built in 1579, but its arcade on slim octagonal granite piers with elementary capitals is early C19. The straight timber entablature (instead of arches) dates from 1863. Original, i.e. later C16, wagon-roof in the aisle. – FONT. Norman, of block-capital shape, with a little rosette, fleur-de-lis, etc., decoration. – PULPIT. With Early Renaissance panels. – MONUMENT. Thomas 36b Welshe † 1639, ten years old; touching, life-size effigy in van Dyck dress on a tomb-chest.

ALWINGTON

ST ANDREW. A big church, though quite on its own. Tall w tower with buttresses of B type, gargoyles and big pinnacles. Nave, N transept, S aisle. Aisle arcade of five bays with piers of A type, capitals to the main shafts only, and depressed pointed arches. Ceiled wagon-roofs. A FAMILY-PEW picturesquely raised at the E end of the S aisle. Its jolly Jacobean carvings, including tall balusters and strapwork tops, were brought from the Hall at Portledge. The woodwork in the church is altogether a most interesting jumble – a real jigsaw puzzle to solve. The PULPIT was made up from bench-ends and wall-plates of the wagon-roofs in 1792, the REREDOS from bench-ends of Parkham Church in 1806. – FONT. Octagonal, Perp, granite, with elementary patterns. – TILES. In the nave, of the usual Barnstaple type. – BENCH-ENDS. Many, but quite a number renewed, and also bench fronts made up of ends, etc. They are in no way unusual, except for the remarkable fact that one is dated 1580. – STAINED GLASS. Small fragments in the tracery of the S aisle E window. – PLATE. Chalice of Puritan style; Paten, made in London 1664. – MONUMENTS. Richard Coffin † 1617 and wife, two frontal demi-figures in shallow relief, holding hands. Below fifteen children.

ANNERY

Late Georgian, the main front with a central semicircular bay with giant attached Ionic columns, the entrance front with Ionic pilasters and a one-storeyed porch. One room inside decorated by a set of oval garland-framed reliefs of c. 1760, coming no doubt from a French or Flemish church (e.g. Joseph and Potiphar's Wife, Martyrdom of a Virgin, Christ teaches in the Temple, etc.). LIMEKILN down by the river, looking very fortress-like.

ANSTEY, EAST, *see* EAST ANSTEY
ANSTEY, WEST, *see* WEST ANSTEY

APPLEDORE

Fishing village with a nice QUAY, many Georgian cottages, some with very large Georgian windows on the upper floor – like studio windows. They illuminate sail-lofts for sail-making.

ST MARY, 1838, by *J. Williams*. Tower and W end 1909. The original building with an E front with bare pinnacles and a very large Perp window between, still in the tradition of the Commissioners' churches. Interior with broad nave and narrow aisles, octagonal piers, low clerestory, and rib-vaults of plaster on little cherubs' heads with spread-out wings.

INDEPENDENT CHAPEL, Meeting Street, 1812. With curved pediment and cupola.

CHANTERS FOLLY, 1800. Overlooking the estuary and said to have been built by a merchant to see his ships come in. It is an embattled tower just like any Devon church tower and now stands alarmingly close to a quarry precipice.

THE HOLT, *c.* 1815. Eight bays, with recessed centre with Ionic columns *in antis*. The ground-floor windows are roundheaded, those on the upper floor segmentheaded.

ARLINGTON

The church lies in the extensive beautifully landscaped grounds of the house. The house, ARLINGTON COURT, dates from 1820–3 and was designed by *Thomas Lee*. The exterior is severely plain, stone, with unmoulded window openings and, as its only external decoration, a one-storey semicircular Greek Doric porch, and giant Tuscan angle pilasters. It does not prepare one for the lavishness of the interior. The whole of the main front is made into one composition with a centre with shallow Soanian arches separated from the side parts by angle columns. Behind this main display lies the Hall, in a line with the Porch.

has a skylight (cf. Buckland House). The large staircase to
its r. was added later (c. 1850). Other original rooms are
the Boudoir and the Music Room (with painted ornamental ceiling).

ST JAMES. Magnificent yew-tree on the s side. The church
was rebuilt by *R. D. Gould* in 1846 (GR) and the tower
in 1899. The tower, however, is a copy of the old tower
with buttresses of type B and polygonal stair-turret. It has
niches for images high up in the buttresses. – PLATE. A
very remarkable piece, a parcel-gilt Tazza of 1552, now
used as an almsdish. Decoration twined vine-leaves and
harpy-scrolls. Also a Paten of c. 1628 and a Chalice and
Paten of 1658. – MONUMENTS. Many, but not one of
importance. Worn effigy of a lady, C14, in a recess in the
N chancel wall. – Gascoine Canham † 1667. – Edward
Bampfield † 1720, small epitaph, but with pretty flower
garlands. – Mary Ann Chichester † 1791, by *Moore &*
Smith of London, handsome, big epitaph in white, pink,
dark red, and grey marbles, with a circular relief as the
main motif. – Mary Anne Gertrude Chichester † 1858, by
Physick of London, with an angel taking the young lady
up to Heaven.

ASH BARTON
2 m. E of Braunton

Fragments of quite a sizable manor house. Gabled range
with mostly blocked or reduced C17 windows, originally
evidently of four lights or more. Behind it two lower
ranges with smaller mullioned windows still preserved.
The main gable carries the date 1665 – a surprisingly late
date for the style of the house.

ASH HOUSE
½ m. NW of Monkokehampton

Late C17 or early C18 house with seven-bay, two-storey
stone front with three-bay pediment.

ASHBURY

ST MARY. Small, aisleless, with w tower with diagonal buttresses and small pinnacles. The rest called 'a modern

church' in 1849. – PLATE. Small plain Chalice and Paten, inscribed 1617.

ASHFORD

ST PETER. By *Gould* of Barnstaple, 1854. Of the medieval building apparently only the N tower with spire – Barnstaple parish church *en miniature*. Inside, a confusing jumble of old bits of WOODWORK re-used as haphazardly as at Weare Giffard and Alwington, bench-ends re-used in the pulpit, Elizabethan panelling in the bench-ends and the vestry. – SCULPTURE. Small damaged C14 relief figure of St John, in the vestry. – PLATE. Elizabethan Chalice without marks.

ASHREIGNEY

ST JAMES. The tower to the N of the nave in a transeptal position (*see* Introduction, p. 16), buttresses of type B and stopping at a moderate height, low obelisk pinnacles. S porch with an outer door having its outer moulding on angel corbels. Nave and S aisle of four bays, the arcade on B type piers with capitals only to the main shafts, the capitals of a concave octagonal form (cf. Chittlehampton). Open, unceiled wagon-roofs in both, in the aisle on angel corbels. – PLATE. Chalice and Paten with date 1610 inscribed; Paten on stand dated 1700.

ASHWATER

ST PETER. The surprising thing about this church is the ancient piers between nave and S aisle (the arcade is of six bays). As they are at present, they alternate between an octagonal shape (buff stone) and a variety of the A type (granite) in which the main shafts towards the E and W are duplicated. The arches are all granite. The explanation is no doubt, that an earlier arcade of octagonal piers was later replaced by the A-type arcade and that this had to duplicate the shafts to tally with the greater thickness of the octagonal piers. The nave is uncommonly wide. The S aisle also wide, with four-light Perp windows. Nave and aisle have original wagon-roofs. The W tower is un-buttressed and has obelisk pinnacles and a NE turret of odd plan (curve instead of angle to the W) rising higher than the tower. The tower-arch towards the nave is tall and unmoulded on the simplest imposts. – FONT. Nor-man, with angle faces and on the main sides tendrils, scrolls, etc., and also on the W side a running animal in a frame with two symmetrical animal-heads. – BENCH-ENDS. Some old, but much restored. – ROYAL ARMS. 1638, large, plaster, on the S wall. – PLATE. Chalice and Paten of c. 1630, but still close to the Elizabethan style; by *I.L.* of Exeter. – MONUMENT. To a member of the Carminow family; probably Thomas Carminow † 1442. Recumbent effigy on tomb-chest with elaborately cusped quatrefoils. Canopy with a depressed pointed arch, double cusped. Inside, the little vault is coffered with diagonally placed pointed quatrefoils. Top with leaf band and big quatrefoil band. The most ambitious late medieval monu-ment surviving in this part of Devon.

ATHERINGTON

ST MARY. The W tower has diagonal buttresses only at the foot and rises without buttresses to an unusual height. No pinnacles. The stair-turret, attached on the S side not quite at the E corner, rises unusually high above the tower. W door with fleuron decoration. Nave, S aisle (arcade of four bays, the piers of A type with capitals only to the main shafts and depressed pointed arches), N tran-sept, lower chancel. Much restored 1884 by *Pearson*, but the curiously un-Devonian window tracery supposed to be original. Original wagon-roofs of nave, aisle, and chan-cel. – FONT. Octagonal, Perp, with quatrefoil panels. – SCREENS. The screen between nave and chancel consists of three four-light panels, each narrow panel with ogee tracery; square top; cf. Parracombe. The screen between aisle and chancel chapel much richer and the almost com-plete preservation of the rood-loft gallery unique in Devon (but cf. Marwood); tracery of B type, ribbed coving, the ribs rising from angel figures, and between the ribs partly

Perp tracery and partly Early Renaissance foliage and putti; cornice of three bands. The loft gallery has thick niches with elaborate and delicate openwork ribbing on the underside of the little vaults of the niches. One of the two screens came from Umberleigh Manor near by which was demolished in the C19. Also from the chapel of Umberleigh manor house, the MONUMENTS. Knight: c. 1250, excellent quality, not well preserved, cross-legged, with a band of stiff-leaf foliage round the whole slab. This band similar to that of the Layespee Monument at Salisbury Cathedral († 1226). The Atherington effigy must be one of the earliest in the country with crossed legs. Knight and Lady (later C14, see her hairdress; the tomb-chest with quatrefoil decoration). Sir John Basset (c. 1530, brasses on tomb-chest with quatrefoil decoration; knight and two wives, twelve children in two groups and shields above and below).

AYSHFORD

MANOR HOUSE. Part of the C17 manor house is preserved, a stone front facing s with several three-light windows. Inside a fine vaulted ceiling with ribbed plaster decoration, dated 1631. s of this front the detached C15 CHAPEL, aisleless with Perp windows and a wagon-roof. The manor house belonged to the Ayshford family (see Burlescombe).

BAMPTON

Small town with a number of wealthy Georgian stone houses.

ST MICHAEL. Quite a large church. The earliest part the w tower with diagonal buttresses only at the foot and a three-light window with intersected tracery. The chancel is early C14 – see its windows (cusped intersected and also flowing tracery). It is a good deal lower than the nave. The body of the church is C15. It consists of nave and n aisle; four-light windows with large simple tracery. Solid plain s porch. The arcade piers inside of standard B type.

with standard capitals. The wagon-roofs are old. – PULPIT with mid C16 carving. – SCREEN, with standard type A tracery and ribbed coving; no cresting preserved. – SCULPTURE. Fragments of panels with small figures in niches, perhaps from a former stone pulpit. – PAINTINGS. Christ carrying the Cross, demi-figures, Lombard C16. – Flight into Egypt (with a ferry and a ferryman in red), good early C18 Venetian. – MONUMENTS. In N wall of chancel extensive fragments of a tomb-chest of a member of the Bourchier family (suggested name Lady Thomasine † 1453). The material seems to be Cornish Catacluse stone (cf., for example, St Endellion, Cornwall).
CHAIN BRIDGE (River Exe), 1½ m. SW. Pretty, early iron bridge.

BARNSTAPLE

Barnstaple received its first charter as a burgh in 930, one of the earliest recorded in Britain. Others were added in 1154, 1189, 1201, and 1273. The town was given the right to mint in the C10, and the same King Athelstan who established the mint founded Pilton Priory just across the river Yeo. Barnstaple Priory, or rather the Priory of St Mary Magdalene, was founded c. 1107 by Judhael of Totnes, lord of the manor. The name of the town makes it clear that from the beginning there was an important market or staple here. The chief trade was of course in wool and also in cloth woven in and around the town. The port was prosperous and remained so to the C18. Five ships from Barnstaple joined Drake's fleet in 1588 to fight the Armada. Visually Barnstaple is easily the most rewarding town in N Devon. It is essentially not a Tudor or Jacobean town like, for instance, Dartmouth, but of the C18. There is nothing individually spectacular, but much unspoiled, modest architecture, and amply enough to sustain an atmosphere.

PARISH CHURCH SS PETER AND PAUL. The position of the church is ideal (between two main streets and yet completely screened from them). Nor has the urban development of the C19 and C20 spoiled the scale of the

surrounding houses. The church was extensively restored
by *Gilbert Scott* in 1866–82 and thus has not much atmosphere inside; but it remains an interesting church all the
same. Architecturally the most remarkable feature is the
tower, placed asymmetrically on the s not far from the e
end, in a transeptal position. It seems to date from the
c13 (*see*, for example, the corbels of the arch towards the
nave with their foliage; dedication of the church 1318)
and is crowned by a lead-covered broach spire of the
second half of the c17, with the bell-openings curiously
placed between the broaches and covered by pediments,
and bells hanging exposed higher up under a pediment-
like little roof. The chancel also belongs to a date earlier
than 1318, but the chancel aisles as well as the aisles of the
nave are Perp. In the nave they have piers of A type with
moulded capitals only to the main shafts, and steeply
pointed, finely moulded arches. In the chancel the piers
are unusual with attached shafts not only in the main
directions but also in the diagonals. The capitals are of the
Devon standard with bands of leaves. Original open
wagon-roofs in nave and aisles, boarded and resting on
figures in the chancel. – STAINED GLASS. e window by
Wailes 1854, w window (1872) and n transept n window
(1878) by *Dixon*. – PLATE. Beautiful secular Standing Cup
of 1554; Chalice and Paten by *Mathew* of Barnstaple, 1608;
two Tankard Flagons by *TC*, London, 1683. – MONU-
MENTS. A large number of the c17, notably s aisle:
Elizabeth Delbridge † 1628 (kneeling figure), Raleigh
Clapham † 1636 (two kneeling figures facing each other,
and small kneeling children below), George Peard † 1644
(good frontal bust, head resting on one hand), Richard
Ferris † 1649 (semi-reclining effigy in relief between
columns, broken pediment above). In the s chancel aisle
Nicholas Hake † 1634 (bust, head resting on one hand; in
oval recess), Richard Jeable † 1643 (demi-figure with
book), Richard Harris † 1688 (with standing and reclining allegories). n transept w wall Frances Horwood †
1658 (demi-figure with head on one hand; the elbow rests
on a pile of books).

ST ANNE'S CHAPEL, to the E of the parish church, in the churchyard. Chantry chapel of the early C14, later used as Grammar School. Picturesque group with elevated decorated doorway, castellated two-storeyed porch and a large three-light window typical of its date.

ST MARY MAGDALENE, Bear Street, 1846, by *Ferrey*. Simple straightforward late C13 style with asymmetrically placed spire.

HOLY TRINITY, Barbican Terrace, 1867, by *White*. The tall tower of fine proportions with large twin bell-openings goes back to *Mackintosh's* otherwise unsuccessful previous church of 1842–7. Dull interior.

IMMACULATE CONCEPTION, R.C., Church Street. In the Romanesque style, 1855.

WESLEYAN CHAPEL AND HALL, Boutport Street. 1868 by *Lander*, plus addition of 1905, both grossly Gothic.

GUILDHALL, High Street. By *Lee*, 1826. Smoothly rusticated ground floor, upper floor with Ionic pilasters and pediment, modest in scale and appearance. Portraits of Mayors and other municipal dignitaries by *Thomas Hudson*, a native of Barnstaple, *c.* 1750 (some of the best now in the Council Room of the MUNICIPAL OFFICES). – PLATE. Silver-gilt Steeple Cup (or Hanap) and Cover, 1589; silver-gilt Steeple Cup and Cover of similar design, 1606; silver-gilt Steeple Cup and Cover, also similar, 1620; two silver-gilt Maces, 1660; two Tankards 1676; Punch Bowl, 1745; Oar, 18 in. long, *c.* 1780.

CASTLE. Only the steep mound remains, close to the present Municipal Offices. Excavations have proved the Keep to have been circular as at Totnes, Launceston, and Trematon.

QUEEN ANNE'S WALK, built as an Exchange in 1708. 43b Instead of possessing four cloister walks around a courtyard as the Royal Exchange did in London, Barnstaple has only one colonnade, but that lavishly adorned. Tuscan columns, doubled at the angles, and in the centre pillars supporting a pedestal on which stands a statue of Queen Anne (cf. the porticos of *Inigo Jones's* St Paul's Cathedral and of All Saints, Northampton). The parapet is decorated with garlands and coats of arms. In the colonnade the TOME STONE, an old stone set up here to serve as a place on which buying or selling money would be placed. The act made the bargain binding.

MARKET, behind the Guildhall. Long hall and along one side of it BUTCHERS' ROW with, on both sides, identical rows of mid C19 shops. By *R. D. Gould* of Barnstaple.

SCHOOL OF ART, 42 High Street. Originally a private house, with nice early C19 staircase (twisted balusters) and restrained stucco decoration.

4 BRIDGE. Probably built originally in the C13. The bridge consists of sixteen stone arches, thirteen of them medieval, the three on the town side apparently replaced in 1589. Total length 520 ft, plus the original causeways: on the W side 1,500 ft, on the E side into town, to the South Gate 300 ft. The bridge was twice widened, the last time in 1834. On the underside of the arches the medieval width of less than 10 ft can still be observed.

HORWOOD'S ALMSHOUSES AND SCHOOL, Church Lane. Founded 1674 and 1659 respectively. S of the church, along a narrow lane with the school as an L-shaped attachment round an angle of the street. Simple two-storeyed cottages with wooden mullioned windows. Small oblong courtyard behind with more dwellings on both sides, like another lane.

42 PENROSE'S ALMSHOUSES, Lichdon Street. Founded 1627. Ambitious symmetrical front with projecting centre and corners. The receding parts have one-storeyed colonnades of rudely hewn circular granite pillars in front which are in line with the projecting parts. The latter are gabled. The doorway four-centred, the side parts with large four-light 'posthumously Perp' windows. A spacious courtyard behind with more dwellings.

SALEM ALMSHOUSES, Trinity Street. Founded in 1834. Three ranges along three sides of an oblong court open to the street. Two-storeyed, of stone, with neat Gothic timber casements to the broad windows.

To see the chief examples of domestic architecture, one should start in the centre, where the Bridge comes in. In

the SQUARE facing the Bridge a large, very urban block of
c. 1840, BRIDGE BUILDINGS, handsomely curved, with
divers Grecian motifs such as giant pilasters and two
Doric columns to the l. and r. of a shop window. The
STRAND to the N has been too much uglified to deserve
attention. In NORTH WALK also, farther N and bending
round the town boundary and the Castle site to the
former North Gate, only minor Georgian bits. From the
site of North Gate SE back to the Square runs the HIGH
STREET.

All up and down the Street houses of the C17 and C18,
often not at first recognized because of the insertion of
modern shop windows, and often not very conspicuous
anyway. A typical example is No. 92, where the pretty
early C18 top cornice with a splash of trophies can easily
be overlooked. Similarly No. 97 has giant angle pilasters
and a nice curved parapet (c. 1700). For the School of Art,
see above. Early C17 plasterwork inside Nos. 69, 81, and 98.
But the best early C17 plasterwork of Barnstaple is in the
WESTMINSTER BANK at the bottom of BOUTPORT
STREET: a vaulted ceiling with broad ribs, cage-like
openwork pendants and the gayest display of exotic
animals. The work is evidently by the same craftsmen as
that at Rashleigh Barton. Two other less swagger ceilings
in other rooms. The Westminster Bank was originally the
house of the Barnstaple Spanish Merchants. Its front
with its shallow bow-windows on three storeys is perfectly proportioned. The same rhythm is taken up next
door in the ROYAL FORTESCUE HOTEL. Opposite the
NORTH DEVON DISPENSARY, c. 1835, three bays,
sedate, with giant Tuscan pilasters. Off Boutport Street at
the near end of VICARAGE STREET the VICARAGE, a
late C16 of early C17 house with original features much
altered, and at the far end the DERBY LACE WORKS,
1796 and 1821 (or 1825?), four-storeyed block of twelve
bays width with little cupola in the centre. Inside, cast-
iron columns supporting the typical fireproof shallow
brick arches. Back in Boutport Street No. 10, PRIORY
COTTAGE, with pretty shell-hood of c. 1710, but

incorporating some scanty Norman remains of the former
PRIORY OF ST MARY MAGDALENE. The priory church
was aisleless and seems to have had a square-ended
chancel. Georgian houses in this neighbourhood: Nos. 9
and 13 Boutport Street, No. 57 Vicarage Street.

s of the Square handsome early C19 developments. In TAW
VALE PARADE a terrace of twenty-two bays with raised
centre, and farther W UNION TERRACE of twelve bays
with a centre distinguished by one-storeyed Tuscan
columns. Then into Newport. In Newport Road NEW-
PORT TERRACE with a raised centre with Ionic pilasters,
46a   and TRAFALGAR LAWN, a pretty composition (no
doubt built shortly after Trafalgar, i.e. 1805). The centre
is a pedimented four-bay villa with Tuscan colonnade
along the ground floor; the sides are of three houses each
with Tuscan porches. The whole faces a lawn or square.
Farther out to the NE in Goodleigh Road, GOSWELL
HOUSE, with long one-storeyed Ionic colonnades.

PILTON: *see* p. 135.

WESTAWAY: *see* p. 137.

BEAFORD

ALL SAINTS. Nave and two aisles. Short N tower (in transeptal position) with short slated broach spire. S porch
with niche over the entrance, openwork cresting and pinnacles. Interior with four-bay arcades of granite with A-
type piers, capitals only to the main shafts, simply
decorated abaci and depressed pointed arches. Fine
wagon-roof in the aisle with cross-ribbed panels. – FONT.
Norman, of goblet form, the bowl fluted and with cable-
mouldings at the rim and between bowl and shaft.

(WOOLLEIGH BARTON, 1¾ m. NW. According to Mr
W. G. Copeland the chapel of the manor house, a detached
structure, survives.)

BEAWORTHY

ST ALBAN. Low unbuttressed W tower with unmoulded
pointed arch towards the nave. The body of the churcl

aisleless, the masonry might be C12–C13. S doorway with two built-in Norman capitals, no doubt from an order of colonnettes in the doorway.

BERRYNARBOR

St Peter. An impressive-looking church, thanks to its tower, and one of some architectural interest. The oldest visible part is the arch between N transept and nave, evidently Norman. The chancel follows, E.E., with lancet windows (E window C19) and a pointed trefoil-headed piscina. The nave is wider than the chancel. Arcade between nave and S aisle of four bays with A-type piers and standard leaf capitals. The last pier but one has two pretty niches for images, one to the NW, the other to the SW. W tower, 96 ft high, with buttresses of type B, a higher NE stair-turret, a W door decorated with fleurons, a large four-light W window with one transome, large niches for images high up on all sides, and projected pinnacles. Tall arch towards the nave. – Open, unceiled wagon-roofs in nave, aisle, and S porch. – FONT. Square, Norman, with scalloped underside. – PLATE. Elizabethan Chalice and Paten by *Mathew* of Barnstaple. – MONUMENTS. Kneeling figure of *c.* 1620, chancel N wall. – Richard Berry † 1645, epitaph with the usual figures of parents and children kneeling and facing each other. – Jane Spence † 1815, by *Stephens* of Exeter, odd, with an oval inscription plate and an urn side by side.

MANOR HOUSE, just W of the church. It was the house of the Berry family: H B on the label stops of the hood-moulds of the four-light Early Tudor windows. Only a fragment remains with ashlar-faced front and symmetrically arranged windows. The porch dated 1634 was transferred to Westaway near Barnstaple.

BOWDEN, 1½ m. S. Farmhouse, containing the precious relic of an original C15 SCREEN, the panels fluted, i.e. with the decorative motif which precedes linenfold.

HIGHER TRAINE, 2 m. SW. Partly rebuilt by *Oliver Hill* in 1939. Somewhat crazy, but after all no more fanciful than many much admired early C19 *cottages ornés*. Stepped gables, a row of triangular bay-windows, thatch, and the garden walls interrupted by tall brick pylons to frame main vistas.

WATERMOUTH CASTLE: *see* p. 159.

BIDEFORD

ST MARY. Rebuilt in 1864 by *Ashworth* except for the W tower (diagonal buttresses, NE polygonal stair-turret, no pinnacles, unmoulded, pointed arch towards the nave). The church is large and wide, entirely in traditional Devon forms. – FONT. Large, square, Norman, with panels separated by thick rope-mouldings. Three of the panels decorated (Maltese crosses, etc.). The whole type is quite out of the ordinary. – SCREEN. In the tower-arch, consisting of Early Renaissance and Elizabethan fragments. – PLATE. Chalice, Paten and Flagons by *W.G.* of London, 1675; Chalice and Paten by *Elston* of Exeter, 1703; two late C17 Tazzas (one is London-made, of 1683); two Straining Spoons of 1739 and 1744. – MONUMENTS. Sir Thomas Graynfyldd † 1513, from the old church, between chancel and chancel chapel, with a fine stone screen. Sir Thomas in armour on a tomb-chest with three cusped quatrefoils (little pinnacled niches between them). The canopy has a depressed arch with large leaves in the spandrels. – Many minor epitaphs.

THE BRIDGE is the *raison d'être* of Bideford. It is said to have been first built by Sir Theobald Grenville in the C14, and the present structure is supposed to date from the C15. That, of course, as with most bridges, must be understood *cum grano salis*. Most of the actual present stonework belongs to the various necessary repairs (e.g. 1638) and especially the widening of 1865. The bridge is 677 ft long and has twenty-four arches (a most impressive structure whatever its age). It crosses the estuary of the river Torridge, as the similar bridge at Barnstaple crosses that of the Taw.

The town rises on the W bank. The main public buildings face the bridge: TOWN HALL by *R. D. Gould*, 1850. LIBRARY by *A. J. Dunn* of Birmingham, 1906. A Quay runs along from s of the bridge (NEW ROAD, HAMPTON TERRACE, entrances from the first-floor balcony; TANTON'S HOTEL, early C19, eight-bay front with raised centre) to the N (No. 8 Quay has early C17 plasterwork inside. MHLG). The High Street runs at right angles to the river up the steep hillside. No individually remarkable houses. The best street by far of Bideford is a little N of, and parallel to, High Street: BRIDGELAND ROAD, laid out by Nathaniel Gascoyne c. 1690. Several good houses remain, especially No. 28, dated 1692 and 1693, the Masonic Hall No. 12, and No. 4 which can boast a fine wide three-flight staircase with twisted balusters. The CONGREGATIONAL CHURCH, spiky Gothic of 1859, is as much an eyesore in the street as is the pompously Italianate METHODIST CHURCH of 1892 in BRIDGE STREET, the continuation of the Bridge up the hill.

Across the bridge is the ROYAL HOTEL, very unpromising from outside, but hiding inside the remains of a merchant's house of 1688, a staircase with rather heavy balusters and one upper room with one of the most gorgeous plaster ceilings of Devon (evidently by the same craftsman as Dunsland), with a wreath of flowers in the most daring relief so that whole flowers are completely detached from the wall, and also with putti and birds.

The wealthy houses of a century later are built farther out and in their own gardens or grounds, especially along the road to Northam: CAUSEWAY HOUSE, stuccoed, with a giant Ionic portico, DURRANT (1810), with Greek Doric porch and a nice curved staircase (Gothic window), PORTHILL (1775?), with Tuscan portico, CLEVELANDS, a little later with a summer house orné (thatched tent roof and raw tree-trunk verandah).

(In addition the MHLG notes the following buildings which seem to deserve mention here:

FORD FARM, s of the road to Landcross. Much altered medieval farmhouse of stone, Great Hall with screen and remains of original roof. Original barn.

OLD LODGE, Abbotsham Road. Early C19 cottage orné with thatched roof and verandah on tree trunks.

WHITE HOUSE, Meddon Street. Built as Workhouse in 1835–6 and attributed to *George Gilbert Scott*; similar to *Scott's* work at Tiverton and Tavistock. One-storey entrance range, main three-storeyed block behind with octagonal centre and pediments to the diagonal sides. Central lantern. Two-storeyed flanking wings.

IFFIELD, North Street. Villa of *c.* 1840, with elaborately barge-boarded gables and finials. One wing with castellated pediment.

BISHOPS NYMPTON

ST MARY. One of the stateliest w towers of N Devon (cf. South Molton and Chittlehampton). Four stages, with buttresses of type B, gargoyles beneath the battlements and tall pinnacles. Very tall tower-arch towards the nave. The interior of the church with thin tall arcade piers towards the s aisle. The section of A type, capitals only to the four main shafts. Large three-light Perp windows, the chancel E window of four lights. The ceiled wagon-roof of the nave is original. – FONT. Norman, square, of table-top type, with four shallow blank arcades to each side of 32 the top. – MONUMENTS. A very remarkable, ornate, Late Perp wall monument in the chancel N wall, perhaps to a member of the Basset family, and probably combined with the function of an Easter Sepulchre. Tomb-chest with two tiers of quatrefoils surrounded by cable-mouldings. The chest in a recess under a depressed pointed arch, the jambs and arch with intertwined foliage; the spandrels also closely decorated.

BISHOPS TAWTON

ST JOHN BAPTIST. The church is small and approached usually from the E. It forms a singularly happy picture with the various roof-heights, and the spire contrasted and set against the background of the grounds of Tawstock Court with mansion and church. Bishops Tawton is indeed in several ways a near relative of Tawstock. The tower, it is true, is not over the crossing, but on the N side.

It is buttressed only at the foot and has a crocketed octagonal stone spire, a unique feature in Devon. The tower has on the ground floor a two-light E window of the early C14 which now looks into the vestry. The chancel arch is the feature most directly dependent on Tawstock. It is unmoulded, but has a moulded sub-arch on head corbels. The chancel itself was rebuilt in the C19. The aisle in its present form is Perp, with a three-bay arcade, with piers of B type and standard leaf capitals. An additional half-bay butts against the tower and opens into it with a fine four-light Perp window. The windows have tall two-centred arches and Perp tracery. Perp also the W door and the frame of the W window of the nave. Much window tracery is C19. Wide original ceiled wagon-roof in the nave. – SCREEN. At the E end of the N aisle, partially blocked, three bays with standard tracery, squarely framed and a cornice with one strip of foliage. – REREDOS. Of glazed tiles in robust Victorian colours. – STAINED GLASS. Much of the time of the general restoration, 1866. – PLATE. Chalice and Paten by *Mathew* of Barnstaple, 1576; Flagon by *Thos. Parr*, 1732; Paten by *Whipham & Wright*, 1758. – MONUMENTS. Lady Ursula Chichester † 1635, epitaph with kneeling figure. – Infant daughter of Charles Dart † 1652, epitaph with a baby in swaddling clothes, 9 in. long, lying below the inscription plate. – John Chichester † 1669, epitaph, still with some strapwork, though with a cornice going classical. – Sir Francis Chichester † 1698, a big, rich, and rather coarse epitaph.

FARMHOUSE N of the church. Said to have been a residence of the Bishops of Exeter. It incorporates late medieval parts, but was castellated and, it seems, generally tidied up *c.* 1800.

BITTADON

ST PETER. Of little interest. Aisleless, low, no more than a chapel in size. W tower stump with modern pyramid roof. – FONT. Square, on four round shafts. – MONUMENT. Epitaph to E. Pointz, 1691.

BLACK TORRINGTON

St Mary. w tower with diagonal buttresses and obelisk
pinnacles, nave and wide s aisle, with straightheaded
windows, n transept separated from the nave by an unmoulded pointed arch, arcade of five bays between nave
and aisle with granite piers of A type, capitals only to the
main shafts, elementarily decorated abaci and depressed
pointed arches. Good unceiled wagon-roof in the aisle. –
COMMUNION RAILS. Jacobean, now screening off the
font. – TILES. With the usual Barnstaple motifs, fleur-de-
lis, rose, etc. – PLATE. Set of 1740 by *J.B.* of Exeter. –
MONUMENT. Very pretty slate plate to Benoni Bamp-
fylde † 1721. The inscription reads:

> Think not his pious Parts have here an End
> No! They to Heaven with his pure soul ascend
> His undissembl'd Love Discourse and Truth
> For Age a Pattern, and a Rule for Youth,
> Unto the Living Charity doth preach
> And Christian Courage to yᵉ Dying teach.

By the same hand other plates of 1722 and 1725.

BLEGBERRY
2½ m. NW of Hartland

(Farmhouse dated 1627 on plasterwork in the entrance hall.
Surrounded by a strong wall with an observation platform and loopholes to guard the approach. *Chope.*)

BONDLEIGH

St James. Norman s doorway with tympanum representing
the lamb in a circle and symmetrical birds l. and r. A kind
of basketwork decoration of the arch. Plain imposts. At
the e end of the aisle two very finely wrought and well
preserved Norman capitals built into the wall. They have
elementary volutes and plenty of small-scale decoration of
squares with diagonals across and dots in the triangular
cells between the diagonals. Norman also the FONT,
square, of table-top type, with large elementary zigzag,
four-lobed leaf, semicircle and blank arcade motifs. The

rest of the church Perp. In the nave tall window in the s wall, 2 lights, one transome. Arcade to the N aisle with piers of A type and standard Devon leaf capitals. The N windows straightheaded with transomes, i.e. C16. The W tower with buttresses of type B and with pinnacles. In the N wall of the chancel a fine TOMB RECESS. On the tomb-chest with quatrefoil decoration effigy of a priest. Above the depressed arch blank tracery of large, matter-of-fact, not at all intricate forms. The whole monument self-assured, but not as luxurious as many of the period. It was no doubt put up at the same time as the chancel E window with its niches for images on the l. and r. – STAINED GLASS. Bits in the tracery of s windows. – BENCH-ENDS. A few, with coarse tracery and some other motifs which seem to indicate a later C16 date.

BOWDEN *see* BERRYNARBOR

BRADFORD

ALL SAINTS. Norman s doorway with one order of colonnettes; no tympanum. The s windows are new. W tower is low, unbuttressed, and has pinnacles, an unmoulded pointed arch towards the nave, and W door and W window of C14 forms. The chancel s windows and chancel s door earlier C14 or *c*. 1300. The N aisle Perp with several types of straightheaded three-light windows and the usual arcade with A-type piers, capitals only to the main shafts, slightly decorated abaci and low depressed pointed arches. Said to date from 1438. – FONT. Circular, Norman, with small fluted bowl. – BENCH-ENDS. A few.

BRADWORTHY

ST JOHN BAPTIST. The church lies by the side of a townish square with several nice humble C18 houses. Wide aisleless nave with N and s transepts of unequal extent, both opening into the nave with unmoulded, i.e. early, arches. The chancel of two dates. In the older part a late C13 s window and a N window supposed to have been the E window originally. Chancel extension *c*. 1400. Of the same date the s doorway and the nave windows. w tower of *c.* 1500 or later. – FONT. Square, probably Norman, undecorated. – PULPIT. *c.* 1700 with open baluster-work exposing the parson's legs. – REREDOS. Tripartite, with handsome elaborate poker-work decoration, C18. – TILES. The usual Barnstaple designs (fleur-de-lis, rose, etc.).

BRATTON CLOVELLY

ST MARY. The church poses some architectural problems. In entering, the first impression is one of exceeding height, but that is accounted for by the evident raising of the floor (see the floor-line of the N door and the rood stair door and the square foundation blocks beneath the arcade piers). The next problem centres round the w tower. Externally it appears Perp, of granite, with a tall NW stair-turret and no pinnacles. But the absence of buttresses and of a w door and the obviously older masonry of part of the w side indicate two building periods. Moreover, to the N a large pointed arch is blocked and a roof line appears above it, as if a transept had gone off the tower in the C12 or C13. Inside, similar traces can be seen more clearly on the s side of the tower, where the s aisle extends as far w as the w side of the tower. Here a double-chamfered pointed arch on the plainest responds opens to connect tower and s aisle. It may be the remains of a s transept, but is not in line with the blocked N arch. The w window of the s aisle is tiny and pointed, with deep, C12–C13 embrasure. The tower-arch to the E is very tall and has imposts of the same design as the nave arcades but with double instead of single-wave mouldings. The chancel is the next part in time. Its windows look early C14. The aisles were added still later. The arcades are in the usual Devon Perp style: piers of B type with standard capitals. The chancel arch is of the same B type and tallies in height with the arcades too. The extremely barbaric head-keystones inside and outside the N aisle windows may look early, but are probably 'folk-art' of the C15. The aisles are both covered with ceiled lean-to roofs, and the nave has a plastered ceiling of very flat pitch. Aisles and nave have old bosses. Externally the N aisle is (as usual) less ornate than the S aisle. The latter has battlements and an embattled W stair-turret (on the N side a similar turret, close to the mysterious earliest, blocked arch, has been broken off). – FONT. Circular, Norman, the Cornish type of St Stephen-by-Launceston, i.e. with faces at the angles and rosettes, etc., in the centres of the four sides. – SCREEN. Only part of the wainscoting of the old screen survives. – STAINED GLASS. Two angels in the tracery of a S window. – PAINTINGS. Remains of a frieze of figures high up on the N wall. – PLATE. Elizabethan Chalice by *Mathew* of Barnstaple; Flagon of London make, 1639; Paten of London make, 1719.

ORCHARD: *see* p. 132.

WORTHAM: *see* p. 170.

BRATTON FLEMING

ST PETER. W tower with diagonal buttresses only at the foot, no pinnacles, and an unmoulded roundheaded arch to the nave. Nave and N aisle not medieval. A rebuilding recorded for 1702–3. Older, the N chancel chapel of two bays with arches apparently of the C14. – PLATE. Unusually good collection: Wine-glass Chalice by *M.B.*, 1591; Paten, 1675; Almsdish, 1684; Tankard Flagon, 1701.

BRAUNTON

ST BRANNOCK (a Celtic Saint, tutor to the family of Brychan, King of Brecknock, who begat so many of the saints of Cornwall). A large and ambitious church in a village obviously of greater importance in the Middle Ages than now. Architecturally one of the most interesting of N Devon. Its most evident distinguishing feature is its Norman S tower in a transeptal position. Visually its charm is the lead-covered broach-spire with pedimented or gabled bell-openings between the broaches, very similar to Barnstaple. The entry from the S wall of the nave into the tower is small, low and pointed. Lancet windows of the C13 occur along the N side of the chancel and two at the E end of the nave, l. and r. of the double-chamfered chancel arch which may also be of the C13. The N transept opens into the nave with an unmoulded pointed arch (now blocked by the organ). That, no doubt, belongs to the C13 too. The nave is now aisleless and impressively wide, but the two E lancets mentioned seem to indicate that there were originally aisles. The nave windows also, although they have now Perp (renewed) tracery, look in their shapes as if they might well be of the early C14. Plain W door with double-chamfered arch. W porch in front of it. The Perp style eliminated the aisles (a very characteristic though rare thing; for the late Middle Ages liked wide uninterrupted spaces), spanned the widened roof by a wagon-roof 34 ft wide, added heavy buttresses to carry the increased thrust, and built a S chancel chapel (two-bay arcade with piers of type B, coarse thin moulded capitals only to the main shafts, and double-chamfered arches). The wagon-roof here is ceiled, in the nave it is open. The vestry N of the chancel, also Perp, has an open timber roof. – FONT. Square bowl of Norman shape, with faces at the corners, but with tracery of *c.* 1300 (probably Norman and later reworked). – PULPIT AND READING DESK. The latter dated 1636. – ORGAN GALLERY. 1619. – SCREEN. Across the chancel arch, four-light sections as usual, but thin shafts and the tracery more elementarily Perp than in most. No coving, and probably not meant to have any. – REREDOS, or rather altar-back, 1563, with panelling, partly plain and partly with simple lozenges, the central crowning segmental arch an indication of the approaching new classical ideals. – COMMUNION RAILS. Balusters of balls of equal size like beads, presumably early C17. – BENCH-ENDS. Also fronts and backs. An unusually large number, interesting also because parish records prove that the number was still enlarged in 1560, 1568, 1578, 1579, 1583, and 1593. The representations include the usual instruments of the passion, shields, initials, whole and demi-figures of saints. There are no Renaissance details. – CANDELABRA. Three, with lovely elaborate wrought iron stars above,

dated 1833, the middle one with coats of arms. – PLATE.
Chalice and Paten by *Mathew* of Barnstaple, 1576; Paten
of 1699. – MONUMENTS. Brass to Lady Elizabeth
Bowser † 1548, small kneeling figure, separate inscription. – Late C16 relief with the initials RB and MB,
against the S wall, panels flanked by three superimposed
orders of short columns, no figures. – Sumptuous epitaph
to the Incledon family, with trophies along the sides and
figures of angels by the achievement on top; dates of
death 1736 and 1746. – Frances Baker † 1782, pretty,
with cherubs' heads, garlands, etc.; not signed.

CHAPEL OF ST MICHAEL, on a hill, ½ m. NE, visible from
far away on all sides. In ruins. The building was Late
Perp, with W porch, W bellcote, single-light N and S windows and a larger E window.

CHURCH HOUSE. E of the church, with old wooden mullioned window frames. Opposite, No. 28 CHURCH
STREET has bits from Perp stone friezes with quatrefoils,
etc. They are said to come from the village cross.

ASH BARTON: *see* p. 41.

BRENDON

ST BRENDAN. Far up in Exmoor, and accessible only on
picturesque routes. Rebuilt in 1738, it is said, from
materials brought over from Cheriton. Tower rebuilt or
renovated in 1828. The tower superficially of Devon type
but in its details clearly post-Gothic. Angle buttresses,
obelisk pinnacles. N arcade and windows of the late C19. –
FONT. Square, Norman, with curved lines towards the
bottom of the bowl, a diagrammatical interpretation of the
scallops of such fonts as Ilfracombe. – PLATE. Plain
Chalice of wine-glass shape, by *I.G.*, 1614.

PREHISTORIC SITES: *see* Exmoor.

BRIDGERULE

ST BRIDGET. W tower of ashlar granite, unbuttressed, with
big cusped pinnacles. Nave and N transept (connected by
a plain C13 arch) plus later S aisle with three-light Perp
windows and an arcade of five bays with granite piers of

A type, capitals only to the main shafts and depressed pointed arches. Good open wagon-roofs. – FONT. Very crude Norman, egg-cup-shaped bowl and shaft of one piece without articulation.

BROADWOOD KELLY

ALL HALLOWS. Architecturally nothing out of the ordinary. W tower with type-B buttresses, S aisle with straightheaded uncusped windows. Arcade with granite piers of A type with capitals only to the main shafts and depressed pointed arches. Unceiled wagon-roofs to nave, aisle and S porch. – FONT. Octagonal, of granite, very elementary decorating yet probably C16. – STAINED GLASS. In a N window; dated 1523. Virgin from a Crucifixion, kneeling man and woman, head of man in medallion. – Jacobean ALTAR TABLE.

BROADWOOD WIDGER

ST NICHOLAS. In a good position on a hill facing Dartmoor. The early C13 survives in the chancel arch, pointed on plain slightly decorated imposts. The tall tower arch may be of the same date. The W tower is unbuttressed with a rectangular NE stair-turret rising above the tower top. N transept (also an early feature), chancel, S aisle and S chancel chapel. The latter was added before the aisle (*see* the confusion between the various arches). The three-bay arcade between nave and aisle has granite piers of A type with capitals only to the main shafts and depressed pointed arches. The wagon-roofs are original. – FONT. Granite, octagonal, with rosette decoration. – SCREEN. With standard A tracery, no coving, and remains, of two bands or ornament from the cornice. – BENCH-ENDS. A large number of the usual Devon type of *c.* 1530, with instruments of the passion, initials, etc., and also some with mid C16 heads. – PLATE. Elizabethan Chalice and Paten; squat domestic Flagon of 1794. – MONUMENT. Knight in armour, *c.* 1500. The legs of the figure are missing. The recess in the E wall of the S chapel where it is placed is obviously too low. The best part of the monument is the tomb-chest with figures of mourners standing under nodding ogee canopies. The knight is supposed to be a member of the Upcott family.

UPCOTT, 1 m. NW. Remains of a manor house, a few mullioned windows, the porch, and a room with a low beam ceiling.

BROOMFIELD MANOR
½ m. W of Jacobstowe

Neo-Tudor, built in the 70s by *George Devey*.

BRUSHFORD

ST MARY. No bigger than a chapel, and not in a village (just by a farmstead). W tower stump with weatherboarded top and low shingled spire. Nave and chancel Norman, the latter with one Norman N window. The nave with an undecorated Norman S door. The pride of the church is its SCREEN, very similar to the screens at Colebrooke and Coldridge, i.e. with straight-topped panels and no coving. The panels filled with un-English flamboyant tracery, and each of the main tracery forms again with the finest filigree of sub-tracery, the bars less than ¼ in. thick. – PLATE. Paten of *c.* 1470, parcel-gilt and badly preserved; Chalice of 1571 by *Jons* of Exeter.

BUCKLAND, EAST, *see* EAST BUCKLAND

BUCKLAND, WEST, *see* WEST BUCKLAND

BUCKLAND BREWER

ST MARY AND ST BENEDICT. Norman S door with one order of colonnettes (volute capitals), the decoration of the arch exactly identical with Shebbear and Woolsery. NE (Orleigh) chapel of two bays with octagonal piers and double-chamfered arches. W tower with buttresses of type B, pinnacles, W door and Perp W window. SE door (reset) with a pretty decoration of branches, leaves and shields covering the main moulding of jambs and arch. The rest of the church 1879–80 by *Hooper* of Hatherleigh. – FONT. Is it C17? – MONUMENTS. Anthony Dennis † 1643, the usual kneeling figures. – Philip Venning † 1656,

small epitaph with demi-figure, frontal, cheek in hand. –
John and Mary Davie † 1710 and 1709, sumptuous big
epitaph. – Edward Lee † 1819, by *Richards* of Exeter,
rather bad, with a small female figure and the inevitable
urn against a pyramid.

BUCKLAND FILLEIGH

Church and house are exceptionally beautifully placed between undulating hills, luxuriously wooded, and with views
towards Dartmoor. In the grounds an appropriately placed
serpentine lake.

ST MARY. Unbuttressed W tower, no W door, unusual
tower arch to the nave, low pinnacles. Absolutely plain
Norman S door. S as well as N side castellated. N aisle of
three bays with low arcade (A-type piers, moulded strip
capitals and nearly semicircular arches). – PULPIT. With
some re-used Early Renaissance panels. – BENCH-ENDS
with initials, etc. – STAINED GLASS. Good Victorian
examples. – PLATE. Exceedingly good Standing Cup of
1599; good Jacobean pierced Dish. – MONUMENTS.
Mary Spencer † 1752, handsome tablet of white and
veined buff marble. – Ann Fortescue † 1815, by *Flaxman*,
of his best, with two men by a pedestal, one kneeling, the
other standing, the sentiment tender and subdued.

37b

BUCKLAND HOUSE, completed 1810, the name of the
architect not recorded. The exterior cemented and thus
somewhat unattractive. On the N side Tuscan one-
storeyed porch, on the main front to the E giant Tuscan
portico. The interior much finer, with several rooms with
glazed lanterns, Greek Doric and Greek Ionic columns.
The detail remarkably sensitive.

MODBURY. Thatched cottage in the grounds of Buckland
House, 1 m. SE, very perfect of its kind and in its position
wholly *verwunschen*.

BULKWORTHY

ST MICHAEL. A picturesque and quite unusual composition : W front with two big buttresses and a bellcote (1873
presumably), S porch with chamber above which is

reached by an open staircase running up along the w part
of the s wall, s aisle of only two bays built against the s
porch. The church is tiny. It is said that an inscription
which has now disappeared attributed the building of the
church to Sir William Handford, Chief Justice of the
King's Bench (cf. Annery) and the years 1414–22. There
are few interior features worth mentioning. Arcade of
granite piers (A type) with capitals only to the main shafts
and depressed arches. E window of lateish Perp design. –
FONT. Octagonal, but made out of a Norman one of the
same design as Abbots Bickington. – PLATE. Elizabethan
Chalice by *Coton* of Barnstaple.

BURDON
1 m. SW of Highampton

Manor House dated 1569 on the frame of one of the few
surviving four-light windows. The house has two far
projecting wings enclosing a narrow courtyard with a
C16 gateway into it.

BURLESCOMBE

ST MARY. Red Sandstone; Perp w tower with diagonal
buttresses. Interior of nave and two aisles with three
original wagon-roofs. N aisle piers of B type with standard
leaf capitals, s aisle of same type but with capitals only to
the main shafts. Three-light Perp windows, the tracery
slightly more richly cusped on the N side. – FONT.
Octagonal with quatrefoil decoration. – ROOD SCREEN.
With standard type A tracery and renewed top parts. –
STAINED GLASS. By *Powell's*, 1858; nice, small-scale representations, though in the usual strident colours of the
time. – MONUMENTS. Nicholas Ayshford, tomb-chest with
figures holding shields, no effigy on top. Late Perp. – Roger
Ayshford † 1610 and Elizabeth Ayshford † 1635, both
epitaphs with the usual kneeling figures facing each other.

BURRINGTON

HOLY TRINITY. Tower in the N of the nave in transeptal
position, SW polygonal stair-turret, the pinnacles on top

missing. Nave and s aisle. Arcade of five bays with granite
piers of A type with capitals to the main shafts only,
simply decorated abaci and semicircular arches. Old unceiled wagon-roofs. The S DOOR original with blank
Perp tracery. – FONT. Norman, square, re-tooled. The
bowl has a scalloped under edge with four scallops to
each side. – SCREEN. Complete with ribbed coving and
cornice with three strips of ornament and cresting. The
tracery of the open panels of B type. Between the ribs of
the coving decoration with stalks and flowers. – COM-
MUNION RAILS. *c.* 1700, with alternating twisted and
straight balusters. – PLATE. Chalice and Paten, 1634;
Paten of 1731 of Dublin make (*J. Wilson*).

BURY BARTON
1 m. s of Lapford

The CHAPEL of the medieval manor house (consecration
date 1434) survives in a precarious state. E window with
remains of Perp tracery. Roof with arched braces. The
Farm is partly early C16, partly C17.

BYDOWN
½ m. SE of Swimbridge

Nice house of 1789 with four-column attached Ionic portico
and pediment.

CADELEIGH

ST BARTHOLOMEW. The W tower with diagonal buttresses
and NE stair-turret has two ogee-headed recesses with
small images of the patron saint. Nave and N aisle are
separated by an arcade with standard B-type piers with
standard capitals. The walls provided with plain white
plaster panelling probably in 1766, when the low BOX
PEWS were installed. – COMMUNION RAIL *c.* 1700. –
TILES. C13 in the N aisle floor. – PLATE. Chalice and
Paten by *R. Osborne* of Exeter, Elizabethan; Paten on
Stand, 1703; Pewter Tankard, 1756. – MONUMENT. Sir
Simon Leach, his second wife, his son and daughter-in-
law. Erected *c.* 1630, the largest of its type in any Devon

parish church, yet cruelly hidden by a miserable organ. Tomb-chest with recumbent figures. The children kneel small against the front of the chest. To head and feet two large kneeling figures, behind coupled columns which carry a coffered arch on which rises a broken pediment. The whole grand, but not sculpturally accomplished. A specially attractive feature is the position against a large window so that light falls on to the figures from behind. – Lady Bridget Leach † 1691, epitaph with large urn.

CALVERLEIGH

t MARY. Of no architectural importance: unbuttressed w tower with polygonal NE stair-turret and no pinnacles, nave and s aisle with three-bay arcade (B-type piers and standard leaf capitals). s Aisle built c. 1340. It has a wagon-roof. SCREEN. Standard tracery of type A in square frames; no coving; perhaps the whole not in its original form. – STAINED GLASS. Pieced-together fragments from St Trémeur at Carhaix in Brittany. – MONUMENT. Mary Coleman † 1636, epitaph with kneeling figure between columns, and behind her three faces in medallions.

CANONSLEIGH

C12 house of Augustinian Canons was transferred to Canonesses in 1284. The remains are very scanty. Parts of a C15 gatehouse with two small two-light windows with cusped pointed heads. Much farther E taller fragments of the Mill. Between them stood an C18 house of which the two wings and the stables survive. Good solid stonework.

CASTLE HILL NR FILLEIGH

ne of the stateliest mansions of Devon. Built 1684, en-larged c. 1730–40, much enlarged 1841 by *Blore* (Stables 1843), and 1862, centre burnt 1934, rebuilt in the original, pre-Victorian form by the *Duke of Wellington*, A.R.I.B.A., in 1935–8. Long plain Palladian front of two stories with a minimum of emphasis on the centre, just the cupola (originally built already in 1684) and a door pediment, and lower straight wings l. and r. Each wing of nine bays, the centre another nine bays. Grandly landscaped grounds with a TRIUMPHAL ARCH facing the centre of the house to the S some distance away, and a castellated RUIN (now completely suffocated by ivy, encircled by a wall, behind the centre to the N of the house). Also, ¾ m. S, a TEMPLE dated 1772, and ½ m. to the NE the so-called MENAGERIE, a smaller Palladian house with attached Ionic portico and pediment. Long beech avenues cross the estate in various directions.

CHALLACOMBE COMMON see EXMOOR

CHAPMAN BARROWS see EXMOOR

CHARLES

St JOHN BAPTIST. Tower (unbuttressed, without w door and pinnacles) and outer walls old, the rest 1891. – FONT. Fluted bowl on baluster shaft, 1727. – PLATE. Elizabethan Chalice and Paten of Barnstaple type; bowl-shaped Paten, 1684. – MONUMENT. Minor epitaphs to members of the Gregory family, c. 1700.

CHAWLEIGH

10 St JAMES. W tower with diagonal buttresses and small pinnacles, embattled S porch, the base and battlements decorated with quatrefoils. Nave and S aisle separated by a granite arcade of 4 + 1 bays, the piers of A type with capitals only to the main shafts, the arches semicircular. Ceiled wagon-roofs with cross-ribbed panels, the chancel panelling and cross-ribbing on a much smaller scale (an excellent effect). – ROOD SCREEN with standard type tracery, ribbed coving and elaborate cornice, the type as in the Exeter neighbourhood. – S PARCLOSE SCREEN. – MONUMENTS. Epitaphs to George Radford † 1667 (of West Worlington) and Ambrose Radford † 1703.

STONE BARTON, 1¼ m. N. Scanty ruins of the C13 castle of Isabella de Fortibus, Countess of Devon.

CHELDON

St Mary. – PLATE. Chalice of Jacobean style. London made, by *I. Y.*, 1636.

CHERITON FITZPAINE

An uncommonly pretty, hidden-away village, with many buff-washed and thatched cob cottages.

St Mary. Red sandstone, w tower with buttresses of type B and central polygonal stair-turret. Two-storeyed s porch with front crowned by nice stepped-up battlements. Star-vault on angel corbels inside with bosses showing the emblems of the Passion. Nave and two aisles; wagon-roofs old. The arcade with piers of an unusual profile: four main shafts, and three thin shafts in each of the four diagonals between. The design is clearly influenced by Exeter Cathedral. Three bays between nave and aisles, then chancel arch, and two more bays separating chancel and chancel chapels. The latter bays have demi-figures of angels above the pier capitals. – PLATE. Set of 1768, London made.

Church House, E of the church.

Almshouses, founded in 1594. Plain, with big chimneys towards the street.

CHERITON RIDGE *see* EXMOOR

CHEVITHORNE BARTON

Gabled, medium-sized Elizabethan manor house, with porch and some contemporary plasterwork.

CHITTLEHAMHOLT

St John Baptist, 1838, by *Gould* (GR). Aisleless, with lancet windows, lancet triplets at the w and E ends.

CHITTLEHAMPTON

St Hieritha (or St Urith, a local saint, murdered by heathen Devonians with their scythes in the c6). The large church faces the village square and the valley broadside. The w tower is one of the most spectacular in Devon, 7a though with its large double two-light ornamented bell-openings rather of Somerset than of Devon type. It is of four stages, 115 ft high, and has six type-B buttresses. Pinnacles on all the set-offs of the buttresses give the tower a fine gradually tapering outline. Quatrefoil and similar friezes at the base and at each stage. The battlements with openwork quatrefoil decoration. Eight openwork pinnacles are the crowning feature. Image niche low on the s side. Nave, two aisles, and two transepts. The aisle embattled with a quatrefoil band below the battlements. Embattled s and N transepts. The windows of three and also four lights. s porch with fleuron decoration in the entrance doorway and niche above. s doorway also with fleurons and a broad foliage bracket above. The door itself original with blank tracery. Interior with five bays between nave and aisles plus two more between chancel and Giffard and Rolle chapels. The piers all of B type, but on the N side with concave octagonal capitals only to the main shafts, on the s side with standard Devon leaf capitals. On the N side, on the other hand, against one pier, an elaborate niche for an image. Farther E, off the chancel N wall, an odd arched entrance to a narrow chamber. It is here that the Shrine of St Urith was placed. Much of the architecture was renewed in 1872 (N aisle arcade piers, chancel with E extension, all windows). In the transepts original timber ceilings with cross-ribbed panels. – PULPIT. Stone, with barbarically carved little figures under nodding ogee canopies in narrow panels with leaf frames. – PLATE. Chalice of Barnstaple style, 1638; oval Dish (secular), 1627; Taster with elaborate handle, 1743; Flagon, 1743. – MONUMENTS. John Cobleigh of Brightley with his two wives, c. 1480–90, brass, small figures. – Grace Giffard † 1667, fragment of large monument, the figure semi-reclining. – John Giffard erected before 1666, standing wall monument with recumbent figure on tomb-chest. Against the tomb-chest two kneeling figures. On the back-wall two bearded heads in profile in medallions, also open pediment, achievement, etc.

CHULMLEIGH

St Mary Magdalene. Though in the town, the church has an unobstructed view to the s over the woods and hills on the other side of the Little Dart river. Proud four-stage w tower with buttresses of B type, pinnacles on each set-off of the buttresses (cf. Chittlehampton), big pinnacles on the battlements, a four-light main w window with a row of quatrefoils at its foot and three-light bell-openings. The body of the church with Perp windows, the walls and window details renewed. Embattled s porch, the battlements with quatrefoil decoration (cf. Chittle-hampton). Nave and two aisles of five bays; piers of A type with capitals only to the main shafts. Ceiled wagon-roofs throughout, the panels in the chancel smaller than in nave and aisles. Nave and chancel with angel figures against the wallplates. Tall granite tower arch, the imposts of A type. In the s porch a square Norman stone with a figure of the Crucifixus in a roundel. The feet of Christ nailed side by side with two nails, not on top of each other with one, i.e. of the iconographically earlier type. – screen. Across nave and aisles, *c.* 50 ft long, very complete, with A-type standard tracery, original ribbed coving, tracery decoration between the ribs, cornice with three bands of close ornament and cresting. The type is the one frequent near Exeter. – stained glass. Some by *Hardman* (tk).

Colleton Barton: see p. 76.

CHURSTON MANOR *see* WEST PUTFORD

CLAWTON

St Leonard. The oldest part is the chancel with one Norman n window. The w tower probably c14; unbuttressed, with tall unmoulded arch towards the nave. Centrally placed polygonal stair-turret on the s side of the tower (an unusual feature in North Devon; but cf. Totnes, Ashburton, etc.). Obelisk pinnacles. Straightheaded n and s aisle windows, with cusped pointed lights. Arcades of four bays. Octagonal piers with castellated abaci and double-chamfered arches. The E bays different (of a different stone too, blue); four shafts in the main directions and four in the diagonals, elementarily decorated capitals and abaci. These bays were probably meant as transepts. – Squint from the S aisle into the chancel. – Good wagon-roof in the N aisle. Bits of wood such as bosses, panels from bench-ends, etc., preserved under the tower. – FONT. Norman, circular, of blue stone with one top band of cable. The base more elaborately decorated with four faces at the angles and half-rosettes on the main surfaces, as if it were a fragmentary re-used font itself, of the Cornish St Thomas-by-Launceston type (cf. Tetcott nearby). – TILES. Some of Barnstaple type with fleur-de-lis, lions, swans, roses; by the font. – ROYAL ARMS under the tower; large, undated, but cf. Ashwater. – PLATE. Chalice and Paten by *Jons* of Exeter, 1575. – MONUMENTS. Tiny brass acquired by a former vicar at Oxford. – Christopher Osmond, 1631; slate plate and above it in relief the life-size figure of a semi-reclining man with columns l. and r., carrying entablature, two allegorical figures and an achievement.

CLAYHANGER

ST PETER. A small church, much renewed. The W tower the oldest part, with diagonal buttresses only at the foot. Nave without aisles, E window with ogee reticulation, i.e. early C14. The chancel otherwise C19. – FONT. Small, the bowl fluted, *c.* 1200 (cf. Abbotsham). – BENCH-ENDS. Many with ornamental and figure designs, the standard Devon and Cornwall type. – SCREENS. Fragments of the former rood screen. – Also fragments of a Jacobean screen (in the tower). – PLATE. Chalice and Paten by *Jons* of Exeter, 1574. The leather case is contemporary.

NUTCOMBE MANOR HOUSE. The present appearance is simply a rectangle with a symmetrical two-storeyed three-window front. The windows of four lights, on the ground floor with transomes, on the upper floor without. Originally the present centre had a porch, the house extended farther to the l. and ended with a short projecting wing.

Gables also have disappeared. Inside, a room with a coarse Elizabethan fireplace with caryatids and a plaster ceiling with thin ribs and pendants remain.

CLOVELLY

The village is one of the show-villages of England. Considering that, it is surprisingly unspoilt. Many of the houses have been rehabilitated and altered by the lords of the manor, the Hamlyns, and carry date-plates with their initials, but the general impression is still on the whole quite genuine. The village consists of an extremely steep cobbled 6 street with a few side alleys. It leads down to a miniature harbour with a curved pier and the big old inn by its side. A small fortification also by the pier. The village houses mostly whitewashed. Many from their style and their little segment-arched hoods on the doors may be dated Late Georgian. The charm of the village is largely the intricacy of the overlapping of houses in all dimensions. It is quite beyond description. The village is surrounded by wooded slopes. Much of the planting is due to the Hamlyn of the early C19, Sir James, who also built along the coast to the E a three-mile drive, known as the HOBBY DRIVE (a remarkable example of the new romantic appreciation of wild nature in her real wilderness, not trimmed to look wild, as it had still been the deal of improvers a short time before).

CLOVELLY COURT. The mansion of the Hamlyns. The old part, i.e. the part built about 1740 by Zachary Hamlyn with Gothic details and classicized by Sir James about 1795, was burnt out recently. Of the Early Gothic Revival features the main entrance with clustered shafts instead of pilasters and imitation Perp tracery survived the fire. The house stands close to the church which is thus half a mile away from, and above, the village.

ALL SAINTS. Evidence of a vanished Norman church is the arch moulding of the outer doorway into the S porch, with zigzag decoration. The low unbuttressed and un-pinnacled W tower also early medieval. Its arch towards the nave roundheaded and unmoulded. The rest is Perp. N aisle arcade of four bays with type-A piers, capitals only to the main shafts, and depressed pointed arches. Open wagon-roofs, plastered behind. – FONT. Norman, of undecorated block capital shape. – PULPIT. Plain Jacobean, dated 1634. – BENCHES. Original, undecorated. – STAINED GLASS. E window with three tiers of small figures, 1885, by *Kempe*; W window with three large figures, also by *Kempe*, 1898. – PLATE. Elizabethan Chalice and Paten by *Jons* of Exeter; Flagon, 1692; Paten, 1761. – MONUMENTS. Unusually many, mostly of Carys, but none of the highest quality. Robert Cary † 1540, brass in armour, the figure *c.* 30 in. long. – Sir Robert Cary, 1586, six-poster type, but the interstices between the columns filled in and adorned with big strap cartouches. – Group of epitaphs all by the same hand, all similar, but no two identical; the dates 1652, 1675, 1677, 1680, 1685, 1686. Another in the same tradition as late as 1728. – Of Hamlyns the following have monuments worth recording: Zachary † 1759, of Clovelly Court and Lincoln's Inn, with portrait medallion against obelisk (the inscription says: 'Exemplarily modest diligently capable, communicative, he acquired a handsome fortune, not only unenvied, but with the Esteem and Love of all who had the Pleasure of knowing him') Very chaste, not at all Rococo. – Lady Hamlyn † 1787, with standing woman by an urn, and Sir James † 1811, with seated woman by an urn, both by *King* of Bath, and both rather busy in detail; not Neo-Classical.

CLOVELLY DYKES. Earthwork, possibly Roman. It consists of three banks and ditches, the banks being 15–25 ft high, and the ditches 20–30 paces in width. The outer enclosure takes in over 20 acres. On the E is an outwork with double bank and ditch; the inner bank is 15–20 ft high. As it is crescent-shaped it was possibly the entrance

COLDRIDGE

ST MARY. Of the Norman period remain the chancel window and an odd blocked pointed arch on the plainest imposts on the N side of the W bay of the nave (perhaps opening into a tower?). It continues E with a clea quoined vertical joint against which stands the impost on which the later arcade starts. It is semi-hexagonal in section. The arcade and the rest of the church all Perp: W tower with diagnoal buttresses and polygonal NE stair-turret, nave and aisles with three-light windows of various but not unusual Perp tracery patterns, arcades tall, with piers of A type and capitals only to the main shafts (N chancel chapel with decorated abaci above the capitals). – FONT. Square, Norman, of the table-top type with seven flat blank arches on each side of the top. – The remaining fittings probably largely given by Sir John Evans whose MONUMENT is in a recess in the N chancel chapel, no doubt his chantry chapel. The effigy must once have been of fine quality. A shield gives Evans's name. The recess is ogee-arched. The chapel is separated from the chancel by a PARCLOSE SCREEN of the same unusual type as at Brushford and Colebrooke, i.e. with Flamboyant, un-English tracery, each tracery opening being finely subdivided by a lacework of tiny Flamboyant curves, the bars less than $\frac{1}{4}$ in. thick. The ROOD SCREEN runs right across nave and aisles. It has standard type-A Devon tracery, ribbed coving with tracery decoration between the ribs, and a cornice with two bands of ornament. – PULPIT. Timber; exceedingly fine in the carving. Flat niches for figures, but now without them. Nodding ogee canopies above and intricate tracery above these, but without any Flamboyant shapes. – BENCH-ENDS. Also given by Sir John Evans; for one bench has a (re-cut) inscription asking to pray for him and calling him 'factor huius operis anno regni regis Henrici octavi tercio', i.e. 1511. These bench-ends with tracery, a head of St John on a platter (Sir John's patron saint) and nobbly leaves still entirely unaffected by the Renaissance, should give a clue to the approximate dating of bench-ends in other places. – TILES. Of Barnstaple make, with roses, lions, pelicans, etc., reassembled in front of the altar. – STAINED GLASS. Figure of a king in E window of N aisle. – MONU-MENTS. Coffin-shaped slab with foliated cross, re-used with C17 inscription. – Sir John Evans, see above.

COLLETON BARTON
1¼ m. w of Chulmleigh

Manor house of the Bury family. Cellar windows on the w side and the back entrance to the screens passage indicate a pre-Reformation house. The present appearance tallies with the date 1612 in the hall. Front of E-shape, except that the E wing is asymmetrically long and low (a converted granary). The main windows of up to six lights and with transomes. Hall with plain panelled screen and plaster ceiling with pendants. Parlour on the w side with rich and varied panelling. s of the house in axis with it a gatehouse with chapel on the upper floor, probably c. 1402.

COMBE MARTIN

5 The beauty of Combe Martin is decidedly its surroundings and not the buildings of the village, a long straggling village, running down the combe to the beach. It was once very wealthy, as the outcome of silver and lead mining. Records of the reigns of Edward I, Edward III, Henry V, and Elizabeth exist proving the existence of the mines. Early in the C19 efforts were made to revive the industry, but failed. A chimney on the hill to the NE is the only visible relic, although abandoned shafts are said to exist in many places. Of the buildings of the village the only noteworthy one is the 48 PACK OF CARDS INN, a rare folly, built on a cruciform plan with a towering display of symmetrically grouped chimneys, eight altogether.

ST PETER AD VINCULA. One of the best churches of the neighbourhood. Proud w tower and proud N front, both in some ways unusual. The w tower is 99 ft high. It has buttresses of type B, niches for images high up, two tiers of gargoyles, battlements and tall, thin, crocketed pinnacles. The bell-openings are specially big (for Devon, perhaps under Somerset influence); three-light with Perp tracery. w door decorated with fleurons. Above it another niche with a demi-figure of Christ, and yet another oddly incongruously E of the N window. The N front is very remarkable. It is symmetrically composed of N porch, N transept and an additional NE vestry. Between these projections the N aisle wall appears with two large four-light Perp windows. The whole of this N side of the church is embattled and pinnacled. On the s side there is also a symmetrical composition of s transept and s porch (the latter built or rebuilt in 1725). These Perp and later additions hide the c13 church of which the chancel with lancet windows remains, the s transept with its un-moulded pointed arch to the nave, and an indication that the w tower reckoned with a nave narrower than the present. As the chancel is also narrower than the nave, the pier at the junction of N aisle and N chancel chapel is thicker than the others, and the designer of the church has made use of this to insert into it two niches for images side by side, facing W. They appear as if they were part of the rood screen. The N aisle is of three tall bays with piers of B type and standard leaf capitals. The N transept has also B-type responds and little concave capitals. The N chancel chapel opens into the chancel with only one arch. Wagon-roofs everywhere (ceiled in 1727), that of the N transept specially pretty with stars in the centres of the panels. – FONT. Octagonal, Perp, with faintly recessed blank arch designs. – ROOD SCREEN. Wainscoting with painted figures (the only preserved example in N Devon). Tracery of A type, coving and cornice new. – PARCLOSE SCREEN with type-A tracery and a pretty cornice frieze. – BENCH-ENDS of the usual Devon type; nothing special. – PLATE. Chalice and Paten of unusual type, silver-gilt, given in 1634. – Big Tankard Flagon, 1748. – MONU-MENT. Judith Hancock † 1634, epitaph with good frontal demi-figure between columns. On the entablature two standing putti.

STANDING STONE, Knap Down, ⅝ m. NE. 5 ft high, with squared sides.

COOKBURY

SEVEN MACCABEES. Nearly the whole of the Norman church survives. The w tower is small, narrower than the

nave, but has odd additions to the N and S, almost like a
dwarfed W transept. These are closed towards the nave so
that the (unmoulded pointed) tower arch is only as wide
as the tower proper. Norman also the masonry of the
nave with two S windows and one N window, the masonry
of the S transept, and the chancel with its windows. The E
window of the chancel is of three lights, c. 1300 (if it is
original in design). The N aisle arcade alone is a Perp
renewal: granite piers of A type with moulded capital
strips and depressed pointed arches. – PULPIT. Jacobean,
altered; the panels probably re-used in a pew. – BENCH-
ENDS. Only a few. – SCREEN. Bits re-used in altar and
lectern. – TILES. Of the Barnstaple designs not unusual
in this part of Devon. – PLATE. Elizabethan Chalice by
Jons of Exeter; Paten of 1770; Flagon of 1777.

DUNSLAND HOUSE: *see* p. 82.

COOMBE BARTON
1 m. NW of Roborough

Tudor manor house. The porch doorway has imposts of A
type (with capitals only to the main shafts), exactly as in
Perp Devon churches. Straightheaded two-light, three-
light and four-light windows of Early Tudor type. In the
hall a large heraldic Late Tudor (or early C17) plaster
overmantel. The fireplace in an odd position immediately
adjoining the porch.

COPPLESTONE

SAXON CROSS-SHAFT. The decoration is mostly interlacings, but also on one side two panels with crosses
saltire. On the same side higher up is a roundheaded niche
no doubt for an image. The date of the cross is probably
Late Saxon.

COTTLES BARTON
1 m. S of North Tawton

Elizabethan manor house, two-storeyed and handsomely
thatched. Porch with the date 1567 higher than the rest.
Inside in the E rooms fine plasterwork, especially in the

upper room which has a pendant and the date 1599 in a
cartouche. Panelling and fireplace with small caryatids in
the overmantel in the lower room. A room at the back
with heavy moulded beams.

COUNTISBURY

ST JOHN THE EVANGELIST. Very high up with views on
all sides. The only feature of real interest is the SCREEN
between nave and chancel, with big, long balusters, a
fully developed cornice and a broken pediment above, all
well carved about 1700. Otherwise nothing more than 200
years old: nave 1796, tower 1835, chancel and N aisle
1846. – PLATE. Chalice with conical bowl on vase stem,
1831.

COUNTISBURY or SHOULSBURY CAMP, SW of the village.
Promontory fort, with ditch and rampart on the E. The
ditch is 4–5 ft deep, the rampart 29 ft above the bottom
of the ditch.

CROSS
½ m. N of Little Torrington

The architectural importance of the house is its fitments 43a
transferred from Stow House near Bude in Cornwall, the
Grenville mansion which was dismantled in 1720. The
house was built in 1680–5, and the large Venetian window
at the back of Cross is thus a surprisingly early feature.
The grand staircase, on the other hand, is 1685 at its most
splendid, three flights round a square well, with splendid
openwork carving in the Gibbons style: lush foliage,
flowers, putti, etc. Other fragments from Stow in other
rooms.

CROYDE
(ST HELEN'S COTTAGE. At the E end a CHAPEL dated by
Mr G. W. Copeland C12. Interesting early scratch dial.)

CRUWYS MORCHARD
House and church are close together. The HOUSE has a
two-storeyed S front of three windows' width with two
moderately projecting wings of two windows' width each,

which looks decidedly end of the C17. An E extension of one room was built *c.* 1682. The W side was rebuilt in 1732. Behind the front one room has a C16 ceiling with heavy moulded beams. No other features above ground prove the documentarily known existence of an earlier house.

HOLY CROSS. Architecturally not out of the ordinary: W tower with diagonal buttresses and pinnacles, S aisle low with five-bay arcades on piers of B type with standard leaf capitals. The unusual thing is the C18 alterations: white plaster panelling of nave, chancel, and aisle, plastering over of the wagon-roofs, insertion of the best C18 SCREEN of Devon, in the grand classical manner with Corinthian columns with correct cornice, addition of COMMUNION RAILS entirely with twisted balusters, simple BOX PEWS and simple PULPIT. – It would be interesting to know the date of the window tracery called with contempt in a report of 1855 'of Wardens' pattern'. – PLATE. Elizabethan Chalice of Barnstaple type; Paten on Stand of 1714.

DAMMAGE BARTON *see* MORTEHOE

DECKPORT
2 m. NW of Jacobstowe

Former Elizabethan or Jacobean manor house with asymmetrically placed porch and two- to six-light mullioned windows.

DOLTON

ST EDMUND. Mostly rebuilt in 1848; but old W tower (diagonal buttresses only at the foot, no pinnacles). Octagonal piers between nave and aisle and slightly chamfered arches. The importance of the church is its FONT, not really a font at all, but two blocks from a Saxon Cross, one square with elaborate and well-preserved interlacings on all sides, the other tapering with Celtic intertwisted symmetrical animals, a human head with moustaches growing into animals and also interlacings. – PLATE.

Chalice and Paten by *Jons* of Exeter, 1572. – MONU-
MENT. Epitaph to Barbara Lister † 1696, stone inscription plate surrounded by elaborately carved wooden
cartouche in the Gibbons style.

DOWLAND

ST PETER. Small, neglected church. w tower with thin
diagonal buttresses and obelisk pinnacles. Straightheaded
nave and N aisle windows. The arcade of three bays between nave and aisle is of timber, the piers of the usual
B-type with elementary undecorated capital strips. The
ceiled wagon-roofs also old. – FONT. Small octagonal
bowl with ribs at the angles. – BENCH-ENDS. Mostly with
tracery, but also Malchus's Ear and the Keys of St Peter.
One panel is dated 1546.

DOWN, EAST, see EAST DOWN

DOWN ST MARY

ST MARY. The most interesting feature of the church is the
Norman tympanum of the s door. It illustrates Daniel in
the Lions' Den. The date must be C12. Otherwise the
exterior has little of interest: w tower with buttresses of
type B and no pinnacles. NE stair-turret. The body of the
church thoroughly renewed 1878–80. Inside, the N aisle
separated from the nave by three low granite arcades; the
piers of A-type with capitals only to the main shafts. –
FONT. Perp, moulded. – SCREEN of standard type-A
tracery with ribbed coving and cornice with cresting,
mostly the work of *Mr Bushell*, the village carpenter. –
BENCH-ENDS. Unusually many, of the current Devon
and Cornwall type. Amongst the representations monograms, profiles, a siren with comb, a cherub with scourge
(cf. Lapford). – PLATE. Dwarf Cup by *Jons* of Exeter, 1577.

DOWRICH HOUSE
1½ m. N of Sandford

Fine embattled C16 gatehouse, the house itself Victorian,
except for the Tudor doorway.

DUNSLAND HOUSE
½ m. s of Cookbury

The E wing Tudor, but remodelled c. 1630, the splendid N
wing c. 1680–90. In the E wing porch, ground-floor hall
(Justice Room) with panelling and a screen partly replaced by one grander of the late C17 (with Corinthian
pilasters), and two S rooms above each other with plaster
ceilings, the one below with thin ribs, the one above
vaulted with broad ribs and little caryatids in the cornice
(cf. Rashleigh Barton, Barnstaple). Another room has
early classical stucco of the Inigo-Jones–Webb-type, probably c. 1650 (cf. Forde Abbey, Dorset). The glory of the
later N wing is also a plaster ceiling, but this one of c. 1690.
Its decoration with garlands and flowers of supreme skill,
the flowers of the finest, completely detached modelling,
as good as any work anywhere in Britain. The fireplace in
the same room at the NE corner equally splendid, with
deeply undercut trophies, a figure of Bellona, putti, and
wild fowl, apart from leaves, etc. In the same wing other
less luxuriously equipped original rooms, some with wood
panelling in the original late C17 staining. The grand
staircase was put in c. 1830 (the balusters indicate that it
was a copy of the original staircase). The exterior of the N
wing is stately, if restrained: stone, two storeys of seven
bays, with a very steep (i.e. really pre-classical) three-bay
pediment. Giant Tuscan pilasters frame the first and last
two bays. Relatively small central door with open segmental pediment. The sash windows partly also original,
i.e. late 1680s, a rare survival. The E wing was in its N part
altered at that time; in the S part it has mullioned and transomed timber windows which look rather 1650 than 1630.

DURPLEY CASTLE
1¼ m. E of Newton St Petrock

Motte-and-bailey castle on a conical hill. Much overgrown;
but the motte still up to a height of 15 ft. Surrounding
fosse. The total area is about an acre. The camp has in the
past been regarded as prehistoric, but is now accepted as
Norman.

EAST ANSTEY

t MICHAEL. Of no importance. W tower with diagonal buttresses at foot, no pinnacles, NE stair-turret. Aisleless nave. Much restored (1871). – PLATE. Early C18 set.

EAST BUCKLAND

t MICHAEL. Of no interest. W tower with diagonal buttresses and no pinnacles. The nave was pulled down when a new nave in the place, where one would expect a N aisle, was erected in 1860.

EAST DOWN

t JOHN BAPTIST. One of the numerous N Devon churches with the tower in a transeptal position. This always indicates an early date. Here the tower is on the N side, unbuttressed and unpinnacled and with a narrow, pointed, unmoulded arch towards the inside. The S aisle was added in the Perp style. Low arcade of five bays with piers of B type and standard leaf capitals; also figures and animals amongst the leaves. Unceiled wagon-roofs. Everything much renewed in 1856. – FONT. Its shaft is the most remarkable item in the church, of wood and with Early Renaissance panels. Foot and bowl are additions of c. 1700. – SCREEN. Beautiful but much restored by *Read* of Exeter. Wainscoting and tracery new. Ribbed coving with Early Renaissance motifs between. Most of the cornice and cresting new. – PEWS. Some, with Elizabethan decoration, in the S chancel chapel. – LECTERN. Odd and alien piece, Spanish, C16, iron, coloured, with dancing nudes on the shaft. – STAINED GLASS. E window 1898 by *Kempe*. – MONUMENT. Edward Pine † 1663, epitaph with two frontal faces in ovals; not good.

CHURCH HOUSE CHAMBER. In the churchyard. The structure may be older, but the windows, etc., point to c. 1800.

MANOR HOUSE, just SW of the church. The present front clearly c. 1700: seven bays, two storeys, stone, with steep central pediment and angle pilasters. But there is a date-

stone 1577, now in a wrong place, and one of the principal rooms has Elizabethan or Jacobean panelling. Also
there have evidently been extensions to the building
which now no longer exist. The house would be well
worth special investigation.

EAST PINFORD *see* EXMOOR

EAST PUTFORD

CHURCH. – FONT. Circular, Norman, bowl partly destroyed.
Originally it was just like that at Harberton. – TILES. O
the usual Barnstaple type (fleur-de-lis, rose, lion, etc.) ir
the s porch. – PLATE. Elizabethan Chalice and Paten by
Coton of Barnstaple; plain Almsdish, 1680.

EAST WORLINGTON

ST MARY. 1879, by *Clark* of Newmarket (GR). Norman
doorway. The outer arch moulding with zigzag rests on
beast's head on the l.; three inner arch bands of saltir
crosses.

EBBERLY HOUSE
2 m. E of St Giles in the Wood

Neo-Grecian of *c*. 1810–20; seven-bay, two-storey hous
with Greek Doric one-storey portico and handsome en
trance gate-screen (two Ionic columns supporting a pedi
ment).

EGGESFORD

No visual connexion at all between house and church.

ALL SAINTS. Away from the village, small and externall
and internally almost entirely C19 (restoration 1867)
Only the w tower old (low, with diagonal buttresse
and no pinnacles), and the NE chapel with a Perp arcl
towards the chancel, the responds unusual with four mai
shafts with big moulded capitals and four minor shafts i
the diagonals. It looks *c*. 1400. – FONT. Norman, mucl
restored. Bowl with rosette on each side and lower edg
scalloped. – PLATE. Elizabethan Chalice and Paten c

Exeter type; Chalice and Paten of 1718. – MONUMENTS. Sadly messed about: Edward Viscount Chichester † 1647, and wife, with two excellent recumbent figures. Arthur Viscount Chichester with two wives † 1674; must originally have been a remarkable composition, with the Viscount standing upright, the two wives lying on the two sides of an open pediment, and tiny figures of children below (attributed by Mrs Esdaile to *William Wright*). – William Fellowes † 1723, plain but noble composition of varied marbles with severely straight sarcophagus against pyramid and niche. Originally four kneeling figures at the foot.

EGGESFORD HOUSE. Rebuilt 1830 and dismantled in 1917. It is now an eminently picturesque large ruin, standing against the sky, surrounded by the woods of the Taw valley like the best of follies. The original building on the site was Jacobean, the early Victorian one was in a Late Medieval style, embattled and turreted.

EXBOURNE

ST MARY. The outstanding feature of the church is its E window, of three lights, early C14, fully cusped, with Dec tracery, but not of the flowing kind (the principle is intersection cut short by a depressed spheric quadrangle at the top), and inside two nook shafts, on them two little niches for angel figures and then above the window a large, bold, cusped and crocketed ogee arch. The whole composition may well be the work of an Exeter Cathedral mason. The small chancel N window of the same date. Otherwise little of special architectural interest. The W tower of ashlared granite with buttresses of type B, hood-moulded W door, and two niches against the W buttresses. S aisle and S porch also of ashlared granite. The arcade between the two granite too: four bays, piers of A-type, moulded strips instead of capitals, and depressed arches. The S aisle S windows straightheaded without tracery, the E window with minimum tracery. The wagon-roof of the S aisle unceiled. – SCREEN. Much renewed, with standard type-A tracery, no coving, two bands of ornament in the

cornice and cresting. – PLATE. Chalice by *Jons* of Exeter
1577; squat Tankard by *J. Cory* of London, 1706; charming plain Bowl by *Elston* of Exeter, 1743.

EXE HEAD *see* EXMOOR

EXMOOR (Prehistoric Sites)

BRENDON COMMON, CHERITON RIDGE, near Farley
Water. The remains of possibly four rows of standing
stones. Four stones stand in line, 18 ft, 15 ft, and 23 f
between them. Heights between 20–33 in. From the
three more northerly stones run rows now marked by two
additional stones in each. These rows are not parallel, bu
run in a general ESE direction.

BRENDON TWO GATES. A rough square of unknown significance is marked out by a stone at each corner and one
taller than the others (38 in. high), marking the intersection of the diagonals. The sides of the square measure
about 30 ft.

CHALLACOMBE COMMON. Between Radworthy and Hol
well Barrow is an isolated triangle marked by stones, som
of which are represented only by the 'triggers' (smal
stones propping up larger stones since removed). The
sides of the triangle are 54 by 55 by 58 ft.

CHAPMAN BARROWS. Chapman Barrows stand on a long
E–W ridge 1,575 ft above sea level, one of the highes
points of Exmoor. Barrows are to be found throughou
the stretch of country to the SE towards the Somerse
boundary. A standing stone 9 ft high, of slate, called th
LONGSTONE, stands by Chapman Barrows.

CHERITON RIDGE: *see* Brendon Common.

EAST PINFORD. A double stone row, consisting of an
pair of stones 12 ft apart, a central pair 13 ft apart, and a v
pair 13 ft apart. In the vicinity are barrows.

EXE HEAD. Between Chains Valley and Exe Head is a
alignment very similar to those of Dartmoor. Its tota
length is 162 ft. It may be the remains of a triple rur
Many stones are now missing. The distance between th
stones varies between 65 ft and 12 ft.

HANGINGS: *see* Woodbarrow Arms.

HANGMAN HILL. On the summit is a standing stone 5 ft 3 in. high.

LITTLE TOMS HILL. The remains of a double stone row. Six standing stones are arranged in pairs about 26 ft and 31 ft apart. The distance across between the two stones of the N pair is 24 ft; of the S pair 19 ft. The largest stone is 26 in. high. Within half a mile radius of this spot are five other monuments including three barrows.

LONGSTONE: *see* Chapman Barrows.

MADDOCK'S DOWN. On Maddock's Down is a standing stone, 9 ft 6 in. high, visible from the Long Lane. It is an unusual veined quartz or spar. Circumference round the largest part 16 ft 4 in. In a field on the E side is a barrow, and around are the remains of many monuments.

TORR STEPS. Bridge over the river Barr, 180 ft long, Bronze Age or early medieval. Twenty loose piles of large stones, spanned by slabs 8 by 5 ft in size.

WOODBARROW ARMS or HANGINGS. Stones mark out a quadrilateral of unknown significance. The tallest stones, 34 in. high, are on the W side, those on the E side are 26 in. high. The sides of the quadrilateral measure 24 by 20 by 23 by 18 ft.

FILLEIGH

ST PAUL. Of the old church the W tower (two-staged, un-buttressed) and the walls of nave, N transept and chancel. Remodelled in 1732 and again in 1876–7. The latter re-modelling tried to convert the church into a Norman building. *Clark* of Newmarket, the architect, also extended the chancel by an apse. This is panelled in leaf patterns of multicoloured stone; the wagon-roofs also have painted leaves. – PLATE. Chalice on baluster stem, 1638; Secular Cup, 1781. – MONUMENTS. Two small brass plates to Richard Fortescue, 1570, both with a kneeling figure; in one he has a long broad beard, in the other a pointed beard.

CASTLE HILL: *see* p. 67.

FREMINGTON

St PETER. Restored and largely rebuilt by *Sir G. G. Scott*
in 1867. The tower is old, indeed early medieval, in the
same position on the N side close to the E end as at Barnstaple and Pilton. Lancet window on the N side, low
pointed blocked arch on the W side. Inside, minor
epitaphs.

FREMINGTON HOUSE. Neo-Georgian by *E. Newton, c.*
1881, but incorporating real Georgian fragments, perhaps bought for the new house.

FRITHELSTOCK

An Augustinian Priory was founded by Robert de Bello
Campo (Beauchamp) about 1220. It was first colonized
from Hartland Abbey. The priory church of which extensive ruins remain must have been built soon after the
foundation. It was 89 ft long and 23½ ft wide within its
walls. The W front stands high enough to show its noble
three lancet windows. The N and S walls had lancets in the
clerestory. This is still clearly visible in the N. On the S
side immediately in line with the W front rose a tower, of
which foundations and a blocked N arch survive. The
Lady Chapel was behind the E wall of the chancel connected with it only by two doors. It was rectangular and
as wide as nave and chancel. The cloister was presumably
N of the church. The present Church Farm lay to its W
and represents a post-Reformation replanning of the
former Prior's dwelling.

The parish church St MARY AND St GREGORY lies so
closely S of the Priory Church that the S tower of the
former touched the E end of the latter. It has a tall, very
tapering W tower with diagonal buttresses only at the
foot, a S aisle of three bays with quite sumptuous arcade
piers of B type with elaborately canopied niches for
images (the first facing NW, the second SW, the third
again NW), and richly carved standard Devon leaf capitals.
The chancel E window is unusually elaborate, early C14 in
the Exeter Cathedral style: three lights, cusped heads,

with a top circle containing three spheric triangles. The two-bay s chancel chapel has piers of A type with concave capitals only to the shafts. Ceiled wagon-roofs throughout. s porch castellated with handsome openwork quatrefoil frieze. – FONT. On circular Norman shaft with vertical zigzag decoration. – PULPIT. Jacobean. – BENCH-ENDS and (which is rarer) bench fronts (with tracery). – ROYAL ARMS. Plaster, 1677, by *John Abbot* (1640–1727). – PLATE. Elizabethan Chalice and Paten by *Mathew* of Barnstaple.

GEORGE NYMPTON

ST GEORGE. Nave and N aisle with straightheaded windows. The arcade of three bays with B-type piers and standard leaf capitals. The W tower rebuilt of brick, dated 1673. – FONT. Octagonal, Perp. – SEATS in the chancel incorporate narrow panels with close Flamboyant tracery, no doubt from a former screen. – PLATE. Chalice and Paten of Barnstaple type, by *J. Coton*, late C16. – MONUMENT. William Karslake † 1769. By *King* of Bath, very pretty epitaph with a cherub standing by a minute sarcophagus against an obelisk.

GEORGEHAM

ST GEORGE. 1876–7, by *Fowler* of Louth, except for the W tower (buttresses of type B, embattled stair-turret higher than the tower battlements) and the arcade of four bays between nave and s aisle (piers of B type with leaf capitals only to the main shafts) and nave and s chancel chapel (same design, one arch). – SCREEN between aisle and chancel aisle, of excellent Georgian design, with Corinthian pilasters and a broken segmental pediment with achievement in the centre. It probably dates from 1762, when the old church was classicized. – SCULPTURE. Unusually fine, though badly damaged panel of the Crucifixion, *c.* 1300, the figure of Christ bent in suffering, as in contemporary manuscripts, John and Mary, two angels above, two kneeling figures l. and r.; all heads knocked off. – PLATE. Chalice and Paten of 1673. – MONUMENTS.

In a recess in the s wall of the chancel chapel cross-legged knight presumed to represent Mauger of St Aubyn † 1294. – Family of John Newcourt, later C17 epitaph with six heads in roundels and a seventh smaller between them. – John Harris, erected 1775, of best workmanship, but unfortunately not signed. Portrait bust at the top, below two putti, busy around the profile medallion of Mrs Harris, inscription below, very well grouped, and displayed to advantage behind the contemporary screen.

GERMANSWEEK

St German. The low unbuttressed w tower with rectangular NE stair-turret is old. The tower arch to the nave is completely unmoulded. The masonry of the church walls, i.e. nave, s transept and chancel, also look older than Perp. Perp N aisle; low arcade of four bays with piers of A type with capitals only to the main piers and depressed pointed arches. – PLATE. Chalice of 1581 by *Jons* of Exeter.

GOODLEIGH

St Gregory. 1881, by *Ashworth*. Perp w tower with diagonal buttresses and pinnacles preserved.

GREAT POTHERIDGE

The house of the Monk family and of General Monk appears now as a five- by three-bay block of two storeys with hipped roof, typical 1660–70 or so in character. The inside possesses two original rooms, the surprisingly grand staircase of two flights with thick balusters and a plaster ceiling with three badly preserved paintings in oval flower and leaf frames, and a large room with a big fireplace and an overmantel with trophies, etc. The room lies behind the staircase, looked at from the present entrance. But this entrance must be later. The room with the fireplace was no doubt originally the hall in the centre of an H-shaped house of which the far half has been demolished (i.e. a shape just like Belton House, Lincs.).

GREAT TORRINGTON

The chief attraction of the town is its position high above
the river Torridge. The fall from Castle Hill down to the
water is almost straight. Of the CASTLE nothing remains but
the enclosure of a bowling green with an C18 gazebo. But a
chivalric past was re-evoked by Lord Rolle in the 1830s,
when he gave the s side of the Late Georgian plain CASTLE
HILL HOUSE a castellated wall with arrow-slits, and built
the TOWN MILLS by the NEW BRIDGE in a similar style
(c. 1846).

The town itself is decidedly unattractive, though it pos-
sesses some attractive individual houses. In CASTLE
STREET close to the site of the Castle CASTLE HOUSE
CAFÉ, c. 1820, with Doric porch and in the garden a very
Grecian memorial sarcophagus of 1818. In FORE STREET
the GLOBE HOTEL, 1830. In SOUTH STREET the lovely 44a
No. 28 of 1701: two-storeyed, five-bay brick with hooded
porch, and inside the hood carved trophies. In MILL
STREET, the w continuation of South Street, the WES-
LEYAN CHAPEL of 1832 with an odd concave pediment.
In NEW STREET another C18 brick house of five bays:
PALMER HOUSE of 1752. It was built for Sir Joshua 44b
Reynolds's brother-in-law, and Reynolds as well as
Dr Johnson stayed here. Height two and a half storeys,
with giant Ionic pilasters to emphasize the l. and r. bays.
The main windows with pediments. A nice original
room on the ground floor, an octagonal gazebo in the
garden.

The centre of the town is the market place called HIGH
STREET. It forms with Fore Street a composition repeat-
ing in its modest way the L-composition of Piazza and
Piazzetta in Venice. At the s end of High Street the
MARKET HOUSE of 1842: three bays, rusticated ground
floor, Ionic pilasters and roundheaded windows on the
upper floor, pediment, cupola. Farther N and reaching
out into the street with 'piazzas', i.e. arched openings, the
TOWN HALL, Georgian, but rebuilt in 1861: brick with
stone dressings, three bays width, pedimented windows

and main pediment. At the NW corner of High Street a narrow passage leads (a pleasing surprise) to the churchyard and church.

ST MICHAEL. The old church was blown up in 1645. Of it remain a low SE chapel with thickly quatrefoiled battlements and the E parts of the inner arcades. The W parts and much of the outer walls rebuilt in 1651, the W tower with spire in 1830. It is a noteworthy fact that the architects in 1651 did not intentionally give up any of the Gothic traditions. Masonry and composition are indistinguishable from the Perp past: nave, two aisles and two transepts, placed surprisingly far W. The interior has an effect of largeness (107 ft long) and bareness. The original piers were of B type with standard leaf capitals.* The renewed piers to the W are shapelessly square with chamfered angles and carry double-chamfered arches. – PULPIT. Plain, late C16. – MONUMENTS. Epitaph to Sarah Gooding † 1698, ornate but coarse. Minor late epitaphs by *Stephens* of Exeter and *Beal* of Barnstaple.

HAINE NR STOWFORD

Tudor house (see cellars) much renewed or virtually rebuilt by *Wyatville*, c. 1810. He added the battlements and pinnacles and decorated the main rooms. In the grounds a cascade and a shell grotto.

HALL
1 m. NE of Chapelton Station, 2½ m. SE of Bishops Tawton

Of the old house only a barn exists. The mansion itself c. 1850 in the Neo-Tudor style with a baronial hall at right angles which, according to an inscription, is by *Philip Hardwick* 'architecton' in collaboration with *Gould* of Barnstaple, 1847.

HALWILL

ST PETER AND ST JAMES. Slim unbuttressed W tower with short pinnacles. The rest of the church so much restored

* In two of the S piers damaged niches for images.

in 1876 that it appears new. – PLATE. Elizabethan Chalice by *Jons* of Exeter.

WINSFORD COTTAGE HOSPITAL, by Halwill Station. Designed by *Charles Annesley Voysey*, one of the best English architects of his time, in 1899. One-storeyed, with *Voysey's* typical almost completely blank gables, a tall tapering chimney-shaft, window-surrounds with irregular blocks of stone, the composition asymmetrical from the street but symmetrical to the garden, with two projecting wings and a verandah between.

HANGINGS *see* EXMOOR

HANGMAN HILL *see* EXMOOR

HARTLAND   2

The parish church, like so many across the border in Cornwall and a few in Devon (Ilfracombe, Dartmouth, Honiton) lies right out of the town, 2 m. W, at Stoke, and close to

HARTLAND ABBEY. The abbey was founded as a college for secular canons about the middle of the C11 and converted into an Augustinian abbey by Geoffrey de Dinant in 1189. Very little of it remains above ground. The Abbot's Lodging was made into a mansion by Sir William Abbott, Serjeant of Henry VIII's Cellar and the first owner after the dissolution. Part of the W front of the present house with an (altered) bay-window may go back to that Tudor house. Late C16 panelling in the entrance hall very similar to that of 1599 at Weare Giffard. Then in 1705 another wing was built which still remains. Some of the windows can easily be recognized in the NW corner of the house. This was built in 1779 for Paul Orchard by 'Mr Mathews' (*Beauties of England and Wales*, vol. IV) on the same site in a Gothic style. The pointed trefoiled arches along its basement fronts, however, are re-used bits from the cloister built by *John Bokerel* of Exeter, *c.* 1325. The church extended farther E than the present house. Of the no doubt attractive Early Gothic Revival forms of the house also not much can now be seen. The E façade of nine windows with its castellation which rises to crown the central three-bay pediment, the window shapes and their Gothic wooden casements, and the library inside with its fabulous ogee-arched fireplace are the only unadulterated evidence. About 1860 much was done to replace the happy gimcrack of a hundred years before by something sounder, thicker, and more solid-looking.

8 St Nectan. The parish church lies higher up than the abbey which, as usual, had chosen a well-watered valley site. The tower of St Nectan, with its 130 ft the highest in Devon, commands the landscape to the w of the house and looks across a mile of fields towards America. The tower is Late Perp, of four stages, with buttresses of type B, gargoyles below the battlements, and tall thin pinnacles. In the E wall a large recess with a contemporary statue of St Nectan. The body of the church, in spite of its size (137 ft long), the crenellations of N as well as S aisle and the addition of N and S transepts, does not look impressive from outside, chiefly owing to the consistently renewed windows. The interior is large and tall. The sense of generous space is no doubt connected with the un-commonly tall tower arch (responds of B type with con-cave octagonal capitals) and the width of the arches be-tween nave and aisles. They date the building as of the C14, i.e. earlier than the normal run of North Devon churches. The arcades are not yet of granite. The piers, though already of A-section, are of buff limestone, short and with simple moulded capitals. The arches are of blue (Catacleuse?) stone, double-chamfered. There are four bays to the nave, one to the transept, and one more to the chancel chapels. A great asset the well-kept wagon-roofs, of all kinds, in all parts: nave unceiled in the w parts, ceiled and painted with delicious large stars in the panels, in the E parts, chancel recently ceiled, N aisle partly unceiled, partly ceiled, S aisle boarded with pitch pine, transept plastered ceiling, S transept boarded panels with carved bosses, N chancel chapel boarded and cross-ribbed in the rich way usual for 'ceilures'. – FONT. Norman, square, highly decorated. The bowl with scalloped lower edge and inter-secting arches above, the shafts with vertical zigzags, the

foot with intersected arches upside down. – PULPIT. The
pulpit bought in 1609 for 33 shillings (with lozenge panels
fitted with arabesques) is now kept in a fragmentary state
in the so-called Pope's Chamber. – SCREEN. One of the
finest of N Devon, the wainscoting as usual, the tracery of
the not unusual B type, coving with unusually many ribs
preserved in W and E, four bands of ornament in the cornice and a cresting of iron. Between the ribs decoration
with flowers and also shields (which is unique). – PAR-
CLOSE SCREENS of 1848. – ALTAR in NE chapel with
some Belgian Flamboyant tracery panels. – PEWS. Nice
plain C18 work. – BENCH-ENDS in the S aisle. Given by
Hugh Prust in 1530. His initials occur on the usual
shields; the tracery also is not out of the ordinary. No
sign of Renaissance ornament yet. – SCULPTURE. In the
S transept remains of small late C14 figure-scenes; perhaps from the back of a chantry altar. – In the N chancel
chapel two small standing figures above the broken-off
top of an ogee niche. – PLATE. Chalice and Paten of 1634,
but of the design used by *Mathew* of Barnstaple much
earlier; two 'Coffee-pot' Flagons of 1698. – MONU-
MENTS. Tomb-chest of Catacleuse stone (cf. St Endellion, etc., Cornwall). Very good and elaborate. Quatrefoil
base, main panels with elaborately cusped and traceried
quatrefoils, roundels, etc., separated by stone double buttresses with little ogee niches between. Cornice with
fleuron decoration. – Helmet perhaps from the tomb of
Sir William Abbott (*see* above). – Brass to Ann Abbott
† 1610, small kneeling figure and inscription. – Thomas
Doctor † 1618, lid of churchyard tomb, stone with metal
inlay. – Several epitaphs of the late C17 and early C18. –
Paul Orchard † 1740 and wife † 1765, pretty epitaph by
Kendall of Exeter. – Nicholas Wolferstan † 1763 and
others, by *Tyley* of Bristol, with Father Time at the top. –
Paul Orchard † 1812, by *Rouw* of London; marble, very
Grecian.

ST JOHN. In the little town. Built 1839 as chapel of ease on
the site of the former Town Hall. Porch with turret on the
E side; the altar faces N instead of E. Typical of 1839 are

the two-light windows, each light a lancet and the two together gathered into one lancet, the simple box pews, the unlearned Gothic reredos, the curious pane of stained glass in the s window. The clock dates back to the Town Hall days. It was made by *John Morcombe* of Barnstaple in 1622 and remade by the same in 1657, when he inserted an anchor or recoil escapement and a pendulum.

HATHERLEIGH

The church lies at the upper end of the town which climbs up the hillside. The market-place below the church with a featureless MARKET HOUSE of 1840 (the town suffered from fires in 1840 and 1846).

ST JOHN THE BAPTIST. W tower with type-B buttresses, a polygonal NE stair-turret, battlements and a shingled spire. Nave and aisles, arcades of five bays with granite piers of A type, capitals only to the main shafts, and depressed pointed arches. No division between nave and chancel. Aisle windows of three lights, straightheaded without tracery, N aisle E window of five lights with minimum tracery, S chancel chapel and chancel windows with Perp tracery. Ceiled wagon-roofs, and CEILURE of one bay. – FONT. Square, Norman, with graceful ogee-cupola cover (C18?). – PULPIT and READER'S DESK incorporate bits from the former SCREEN. – At the w end of the s aisle a PEW incorporating Jacobean panels. – BENCH-ENDS with the usual foliage decoration. – COMMUNION RAILS with alternating fluted and twisted balusters. – STAINED GLASS. Flemish C17 bits in the s aisle w window. – PLATE. Large Cup on baluster stem by *Freeman* of Exeter, 1701; Wine Bottle with inscription of 1722; plain Paten on stand, 1731; Flagon by *Whipham & Wright* of London, 1797.

OBELISK, 1 m. w. Erected in 1860 to commemorate Lt.-Col. Morris.

HEANTON PUNCHARDON

ST AUGUSTINE. Quite impressively placed along the hillside overlooking the estuary of the river Taw. The feature

Scenery: Valley of the Rocks, near Lynton

Scenery: Rocky coast, Hartland Quay

Scenery: Exmoor, near Simonsbath

3

Town and River: Barnstaple Bridge and the river Taw

4

Village in a Combe: Combe Martin

Village Street: Clovelly

(b) *Church Exteriors*: Chittlehampton, Tower

(a) *Church Exteriors*: Frithelstock Priory, east end, thirteenth century

7

Church Exteriors: Hartland

Church Interiors: Tawstock, early fourteenth century, probably a remodelling of Norman walls

Church Interiors: Chawleigh, fifteenth century

Church Interiors: Molland, fifteenth century, with later 'tympanum'

Church Interiors: The roof of Northlew Church

Church Interiors: Detail from the roof of Northlew Church

Decoration in Stone: Dolton, fragments of a Saxon Cross
now used as a font

Decoration in Stone: Bondleigh, Norman capital

(a) *Decoration in Stone:* Exbourne, early fourteenth-century tracery

(b) *Decoration in Stone:* Swimbridge, fifteenth-century capital

(a) *Church Furnishings in Stone:* North Molton, Font, fifteenth century

(b) *Church Furnishings in Wood:* North Molton, Panelling in the Chancel, seventeenth century

Church Furnishings in Wood: Swimbridge, Rood screen

Church Furnishings in Wood: Atherington, Rood screen,
detail from the loft

Church Furnishings in Wood: Atherington, Rood screen, detail

(b) *Church Furnishings in Wood*: Swimbridge,
Rood screen, Canopy of a lay altar

(a) *Church Furnishings in Wood*: Brushford,
Rood screen

Church Furnishings in Wood: Lapford, Rood screen, detail of the coving, *c.* 1540

(b) *Church Furnishings in Wood*: Washfield,
Rood screen, 1624

(a) *Church Furnishings in Wood*: Tawstock,
Pew, c. 1540-50

23

(a) *Church Furnishings in Wood:* Holcombe Rogus, Bluett Pew,
early seventeenth century

(b) *Church Furnishings in Wood:* Cruwys Morchard, Rood screen,
early eighteenth century

Church Furnishings in Wood: Swimbridge, Font cover, *c.* 1540

(a) *Church Furnishings in Wood*: Pilton, Font cover, sixteenth-century work of various dates

(b) *Church Furnishings in Wood*: Atherington, Benches, fifteenth century

Church Furnishings in Wood: High Bickington, Benches, early sixteenth century

(a) *Church Furnishings in Wood:* Braunton, Bench-end with Instruments of the Passion

(b) *Church Furnishings in Wood:* Lapford, Bench-end, c. 1530

28

Church Furnishings in Wood: Warkleigh, Bench front of *c.* 1540–50, re-used

(a) Warkleigh: Wooden Pyx Case,
c. fifteenth century

(b) *Church Monuments:* Monkleigh, Sir William Hankford † 1422

Church Monuments: Heanton Punchardon, Richard Coffin † 1523

Church Monuments: Bishops Nympton, fifteenth century

Church Monuments: Pilton, Sir John Chichester † 1569

Church Monuments: Tawstock, Frances Lady Fitzwarren † 1589

Church Monuments: Landkey, Sir Arthur Acland † 1610

(a) *Church Monuments*: Tawstock, William Bourchier,

(b) *Church Monuments*: Alverdiscott, Thomas Welshe †: 1639

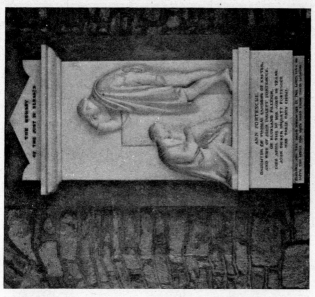

(a) *Church Monuments*: Tawstock, Lady Rachel Fane, wife of the fifth Earl of Bath, † 1680

(b) *Church Monuments*: Buckland Filleigh, Ann Fortescue † 1815, by John Flaxman

Domestic Architecture: Weare Giffard, Hall, hammerbeam roof, late
fifteenth century (*Copyright Country Life*)

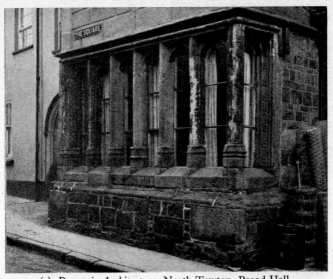

(a) *Domestic Architecture:* North Tawton, Broad Hall, fifteenth-century bay window

(b) *Domestic Architecture:* Tawstock Court, Gatehouse, 1574

Domestic Architecture: Holcombe Court, Gatehouse, *c.* 1525
(*Copyright Country Life*)

Domestic Architecture: Barnstaple, Plaster ceiling in the former house of the
Spanish Merchants, c. 1620

Domestic Architecture: Barnstaple, Penrose's Almshouses, *c.* 1627

(a) *Domestic Architecture*: Cross near Great Torrington, staircase from Stow, c. 1685

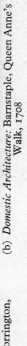

(b) *Domestic Architecture*: Barnstaple, Queen Anne's Walk, 1708

43

(b) *Domestic Architecture:* Great Torrington,
Palmer House, 1752

(a) *Domestic Architecture:* Great Torrington,
House of 1701 in South Street

Domestic Architecture: Tawstock Court, c. 1790

45

(a) *Domestic Architecture:* Barnstaple, Trafalgar Lawn, *c.* 1805–10

(b) *Domestic Architecture:* Ilfracombe, Tunnel Baths, 1836

(a) *Domestic Architecture:* Arlington Court, 1820–3, by Thomas Lee

(b) *Domestic Architecture:* Knightshayes, near Tiverton, 1870–3,
by William Burges

47

Combe Martin: The Pack of Cards Inn

which will be remembered is the arcade between nave and N aisle, with the usual Devon piers of B type placed not diagonally but so that they form square piers. They are placed on square blocks. Very thin cornices rather than capitals are added, and depressed arches. Is it a re-management of Perp parts in the C19? The arcade is five bays long. The aisle windows are straightheaded, Late Perp, with no tracery. Aisle as well as nave have the original wagon-roofs ceiled. The tall W tower has buttresses of type B, and unusually big three-light bell-openings. – FONT. Octagonal, without datable features, on five shafts. – SCREEN. Much restored, especially in the coving. The tracery is type A standard. – PLATE. Elizabethan Chalice and Paten by *Mathew* of Barnstaple; two Patens and a Tankard Flagon, 1714. – MONUMENTS. Richard Coffin † 1523, extremely elaborately yet somewhat rustically decorated recess in the chancel N wall, the decoration almost exclusively Perp foliage, no tracery or similar geometrical elements. And even on the tomb-chest, where there are two tiers of quatrefoils, they have frames of leaves and leaves in the spandrels. The usual depressed pointed arch covers the recess; the cresting again with foliage; also a centrally placed little figure of an angel. No effigy. – Bassett monuments in the NE chapel: Elizabeth † 1635, epitaph with the usual kneeling figure; Arthur † 1672, good example of its date; John † 1683, etc.

HEANTON COURT. The house in its present form with battlements and Georgian windows looks *c.* 1790. It lies below the village by the estuary.

PREHISTORIC STONE. In the second hedge below Wratton House, almost rectangular, perhaps moved from its original position.

HEANTON SATCHVILLE

The mansion was recently burnt down completely and re-erected on a smaller scale, in an adaptation of the William-and-Mary style, by *Sir Walter Tapper*.

HEMBURY CAMP (or CASTLE)
2 m. s Buckland Brewer

Neolithic hill-camp with a small rising in the centre, perhaps the remains of a burial mound. The camp is roughly rectangular and enclosed by banks and ditches.

HIGHAMPTON

HOLY CROSS. Outside the village. Norman s door with one order of colonnettes with very curious somewhat dubious capitals. Unbuttressed, pinnacled w tower; nave and N aisle with straightheaded windows, the individual lights pointed and cusped. The aisle is separated from the nave by two tall shapeless granite columns of 1834 carrying the wallplate of the old nave wagon-roof. The chancel also of 1834. – FONT. Norman, of the Cornish Fowey type with a small bowl adorned at the top by a broad band of simple motifs such as crosses saltire, starts, etc. – PLATE. Elizabethan Chalice and Paten by *R.H.* of Exeter.

BURDON: *see* p. 65.

HIGH BICKINGTON

ST MARY. Of the Norman church the s door remains (with moderate zigzag decoration of the arches, one beast's-head corbel, and one order of colonnettes in the jambs and the lower storeys of a former s tower in transepta position. The arch into the nave is pointed and unmoulded. A w tower was built instead in the Perp style tall, of three stages, with diagonal buttresses and shor pinnacles. The rest of the church later. Nave and N aisle The arcade of 4+2 bays, the two easternmost pier octagonal, the arches simply moulded. The four w pier of A type with capitals only to the main shafts. Th SEDILIA with ogee arches point to the early C14, whicl may also be the date of the octagonal piers. Nave, N aisl and w tower all Perp. Original ceiled wagon-roofs.

FONT. Norman, square, like a large block-capital. Th semicircular surfaces decorated with large wheels, rosette and crosses, two motifs to each side. – BENCH-ENDS c. 70, a collection of a size unique in North Devon. The

27

can easily be divided into different types: tracery, pairs of saints or prophets, Instruments of the Passion, initials in shields, Renaissance foliage, Renaissance profiles in medallions, putti blowing trumpets. – PLATE. London-made Chalice and Paten, 1599.

HIGHBRAY

ALL SAINTS. High up in an exposed position with beautiful views to the S and N (towards Exmoor). Broad, not tall, W tower with buttresses of type B, gargoyles and human heads below the battlements and short obelisk pinnacles. NE polygonal stair-turret. N and S windows straight-headed. Low arcade of four bays between nave and S aisle. B piers and standard leaf capitals. Ceiled wagon-roofs without bosses. – FONT. Norman, circular, with one shallow zigzag frieze, and on the collar palmettes. – SCREEN. Only three sections remain (in the tower arch) with standard type-A tracery.

HIGHER TRAINE see BERRYNARBOR

HOLCOMBE ROGUS

Holcombe Court and the church form an uncommonly attractive group on the hill, close together yet separated by a wall with a circular dovecote. The village climbs up to house and church.

ALL SAINTS. Perp throughout. Nave and two aisles, chancel and two chancel chapels. W tower with buttresses of type B. Three-light windows, except for the five-light window of the N chancel chapel, which is the Bluett family chapel. The Bluetts built Holcombe Court and held the manor to the middle of the C19. The nave arcades with piers of standard B type, on the S with capitals only to the four main shafts, on the N with standard Devon leaf capitals. One S pier with a diagonally placed niche for an image. The N aisle with wagon-roof unceiled, the S aisle ceiled. S porch with graceful fan-vault and graceful arcading outside above the entrance. – SCREEN. Brought from St Peter's, Tiverton. B type, unusual in the pretty

motif of scrolls or ribbons in the head lozenges of the
24a tracery. – BLUETT PEW. A rare example of a completely
preserved Jacobean family pew. The screen partitions off
part of the N aisle. Balusters, and on top small relief
medallions with scenes from the early parts of Genesis. –
PAINTING. Oblong, Venetian, c. 1600, with the Virgin
surrounded by saints and Venetian nobility. – PLATE.
Large Puritan-style Chalice and Paten of 1633–4; Paten
on foot of 1700–1; Tankard Flagon of 1771–2. – MONU-
MENTS. Richard Bluett † 1614 and wife, alabaster under
shallow coffered arch; recumbent figure of woman, the
man a little higher, behind her, semi-reclining on one
elbow; good cartouche on the back wall; small allegorical
figures on the cornice above the columns which support
the arch. – Sir John Bluett † 1634 and wife, also alabaster,
under heavy pediment; both figures recumbent, she
behind and a little higher; eight children kneeling against
the front of the tomb-chest. – The Rev. Robert Bluett †
1749, excellent, grand and sober, very metropolitan-look-
ing epitaph with urn in aedicule high up. On the pedestal
of the urn a large relief of the Good Samaritan (by
whom?). – Robert and Kerenhappuch Bluett, erected
1783, by *Mauge & Co.* of Bath (an early case no doubt of
the use of '& Co.' for a sculptor's workshop), epitaph with
two seated allegories by an urn high above inscription
plate. – Several minor C18 monuments.

40 HOLCOMBE COURT. The front is the most spectacular
piece of Early Tudor domestic architecture in Devon. Its
date is c. 1520–30. It is asymmetrical with a big buttressed
tower over the entrance and a broad and high stair-turret
to its l. (not the more formal arrangement with symmetrical angle turrets as, for example, Hampton Court
and so many other Tudor gatehouses). The tower
windows are original, those of the hall on the r. of the
tower (six lights with transomes) and the others in that
part of the house are late C16, perhaps connected with
work going on in 1591. To the r. of the front a big circular
dovecote with conical roof, also C16. The front faces S;
the NW wing was pulled down in 1845, and extensive re-

building took place, especially at the back, in 1858–9. The inner courtyard behind the hall is, however, original at least in its position. Of the interiors the hall has an 1858 screen, but the original doors from the screens' passage to the offices. The hall ceiling is said to be of 1858 also, but has the same style, with thin ribs forming star or cross patterns, as the original dining-room ceiling. Originally a large window such as those towards the front opened from the hall into the courtyard as well. The main staircase starts from the hall and projects into the courtyard. The dining-room to the E of the hall has wood panelling and a timber fireplace of comparatively restrained character. The bay-window seems removed. In the study is a re-used ceiling with heavy moulded beams and elaborately decorated bosses, obviously going back to the first building period of the house. On the first floor the drawing-room has a chimneypiece with caryatids and the date 1591, and the ceiling curved ribs, as thin as those on the ground floor. The chimneypiece in the bedroom above the dining-room has a far from attractive relief of the Brazen Serpent between caryatids. On the second floor a gallery, 65 ft long, runs all along the front. Its plaster ceiling is again of the same style as the others. C16 panelling in the rooms as well. – Fine grounds, landscaped and with a serpentine lake.

HOLLACOMBE

ᵗ PETROCK. An aisleless church; the W tower low, unbuttressed, with saddleback roof; no W door (i.e. all early features). The S side of the nave has a lancet window and a very plain Norman doorway. The lintel stone has a sloping pediment-like top and is decorated with three big rosettes, such as they often appear on fonts.* The chancel E window is of two lights with a circle above the cusped heads of the lights (i.e. late C13). The (renewed) chancel S window goes well with that date. – FONT. Octagonal, inside the church; another, square, Norman, on five shafts, outside the porch. – READING DESK with some

* Above it a badly preserved top of a lantern-cross.

re-used balusters. – PLATE. Cup of 1573–4 by *Jons* of
Exeter.

HOLSWORTHY

The town has singularly little to appeal to the visitor. The
church lies at the E end, a little away from the centre and
with its N side still as close to the fields as if it were a village
church.

St PETER AND St PAUL. The W tower is stately, of a type
familiar in Devon: ashlar granite, with buttresses of B
type, pinnacles on their off-sets (cf. Chittlehampton, etc.)
and hefty cusped pinnacles. The rest of the church is so
much restored that it appears to be C19. Evidence of a
Norman church is afforded by two stones in the S porch:
one is a capital of a colonnette, the other the centre of a
tympanum, showing the lamb carrying the cross. The
interior has five-bay arcades to the N and S. The piers are
octagonal, the arches double-chamfered. The chancel
dates from 1880–2, the N aisle was rebuilt in 1884. The
general impression in the church is throughout of Victorian work. – Old bits incorporated in several pieces of
furniture: fragments of COMMUNION RAILS with twisted
balusters, an openwork carved PANEL of *c.* 1710, BENCH-
ENDS. – STAINED GLASS. N aisle W window by *Bell* of
Great Russell Street, 1876; E window by *Lavers & West-
lake, c.* 1882. – PLATE. Exeter-type Chalice and Paten of
1576; Paten, 1778; good brass Almsdish.

HONEYCHURCH

St JAMES. Two Norman beast heads (from a corbel
table?) walled into the S wall of the nave indicate the
existence of a Norman church the plan of which remains
probably unchanged, except for the Perp W tower with
type-B buttresses, a low rectangular NE stair-turret and
pinnacles. The nave has now straightheaded three-light
windows without tracery. In the N wall a niche seems a
re-used Norman window. The chancel is lower than the
nave; the chancel arch with imposts of A type. Wagon
roof in the nave. – FONT. Norman, circular, coarse zigzag

and cable decoration. – BENCH-ENDS. Elementarily decorated. – COMMUNION RAILS. Baluster type. – PLATE. Elizabethan Chalice and Paten of Exeter type, by *R. Osborn.*

HORWOOD

ST MICHAEL. The plan as usual in this part of Devon, one side still with transept and aisleless (S), the other with an added Perp aisle (N). The chancel belongs to the earlier period (*see* the piscina with an odd horn-shaped drain). Arcade of five bays, low piers of B type with standard capitals and depressed pointed arches. Bosses and wall-plates of the aisle roof original. W tower low, unbuttressed, with small pinnacles, and unmoulded round-headed arch to the nave. – FONT. Norman, square, with scalloped under edge. – PULPIT. 1635 with tall, slim, restrained panels (blank arcades with lozenges, etc., in them); wholly pre-classical. – SCREEN. A few fragments displayed on the S wall. – BENCH-ENDS. Shields, etc., as usual, also two saints; not yet any Renaissance features. – COMMUNION RAIL in chancel chapel, Jacobean. – TILES. In the chancel; of the usual Barnstaple patterns. – STAINED GLASS. C15 figures in the tracery of the N aisle E window. – PLATE. Elizabethan Chalice and Paten by *T. Mathew* of Barnstaple. – MONUMENT. Mid C15 alabaster monument to a lady, horned headdress, small figures of children under her cloak, on the pattern of representations of the Virgin of Misericord; not very well preserved.

HUISH

ST JAMES THE LESS. Old, small, unbuttressed W tower. The rest of the church 1873 by *Street,* and not of his best. – PLATE. Elizabethan Chalice.

HEANTON SATCHVILLE: see p. 97.

HUNTSHAM

ALL SAINTS. Slim unbuttressed W tower. Nave with a N aisle added in 1871. – SCREEN. Small bits re-used as altar-back. – STAINED GLASS, by *Wailes, c.* 1856.

HUNTSHAM COURT. 1869, by *Ferrey*; it is said, on the pattern of the pre-existing mansion. Some of the old oak panelling re-instated in the hall.

HUNTSHAW

ST MARY MAGDALENE. Handsome arcade between nave and N aisle. Piers of B type with standard capitals, having figures (e.g. a tumbler in an unseemly posture) between the leaves, and with niches for images on the first pier facing SW, on the second NW, on the third again SW (cf. Frithelstock). Wagon-roof in the nave. W tower with diagonal buttresses and no pinnacles. All this may be connected with the indulgence of 1439 to those who would help in the rebuilding of Huntshaw Church. Only the chancel is considerably older (*see* the S window of *c.* 1300). – TILES. In the chancel, of the usual Barnstaple patterns. – PLATE. Chalice and Paten by *I.P.*, London, 1573–4. – MONUMENT. Rich epitaph to Thomas Saltren † 1700.

IDDESLEIGH

ST JAMES. W tower with diagonal buttresses, a W door with elaborate, though badly preserved leaf decoration, gargoyles, granite battlements and tiny pinnacles. Nave, N aisle, lower chancel, and S porch. Tall arcade of four bays with piers of A type and capitals only to the main shafts. Unceiled wagon-roofs. – FONT. Octagonal, Perp, with very plain decoration. Jacobean cover. – PULPIT. C17, panelled, with strapwork. – SCREEN. Only three divisions remain, with tracery of B type; no coving or cornice. – PLATE. Chalice and Paten by *HC* of London, 1576. – MONUMENT. Cross-legged knight in low arched recess in the N chancel chapel. Late C13. – Slate plate to Wilmot Veale † 1681.

ILFRACOMBE

To-day Ilfracombe is the most popular seaside resort of N Devon. Up to the end of the Georgian era it was a small fishing town, with the parish church well over half a mile away on a hill (very much as at Honiton, Dartmouth and in other Devon towns). Efforts to attract seaside visitors seem to have begun about 1830, but success came only with the High Victorian days, and the architecture of Ilfracombe is dominated by the houses of the last third of the C19.

HOLY TRINITY. The oldest part is the tower, in the N transeptal position, frequent in early N Devon churches. It is low and unbuttressed, and has a simple pointed N door, a lancet window to the N and a low unmoulded pointed arch to the S into the church. Then, in 1321, Bishop Stapledon commanded that the church should be enlarged, by a lengthening of the nave and the addition of aisles. The present N and S aisle arcades of four bays to the tower do in fact go well with a date in the second quarter of the C14: low octagonal piers and simply chamfered arches. Of the same date the piscina in the chancel. In the early C15 a N chancel chapel was added with piers of B type and simple fairly big moulded capitals only to the main shafts. The aisle windows, and probably the whole widening of the aisles to their present size, appears to be later Perp still, though most of the outer walls was rebuilt in the C19. Of the C19 entirely the arcade of the S chancel chapel and the E part of the N chancel chapel. The windows with their tracery were then also renewed. The chancel E window is C19. It was Perp like the E windows to the N and S aisles, as is shown in old illustrations. These windows are of four lights, and so are those of the N and S sides, i.e. the church was on an ambitious scale all round. The wagon-roofs are specially rewarding at Holy Trinity. They are all ceiled. In the nave the beams rest on angel figures, and below these are gargoyles. At the E end of the nave, i.e. above the former rood screen, is a splendid *ceilure* or Glory, three bays enriched by cross-ribs and much decoration. To make this and the screen better visible two dormer windows are inserted, one N, one S. These were remade in 1899 (*Fellowes Prynne*), but must have existed at least as early as the mid C18, and so probably are an original feature. The chancel roof with its own *ceilure* (cf. Swimbridge) is new. The N porch alone has an open wagon-roof. – The LYCHGATE and also the VESTRY were added by *H. Wilson*, Sedding's best pupil. – FONT. Square, Norman, with scalloped underside and a decoration of three rosettes on each side. – PULPIT. Elizabethan with two tiers of the characteristic arched panels on short columns; flowers with stalks and leaves as the motif within each panel. – S DOOR. Original, with its knocker. – STAINED GLASS. 1861, E window by *Hardman*, S aisle E window by *Willement*, window in N wall just w of tower by *Lavers & Barraud*; 1862, N aisle E window by *O'Connor*; 1866, Stabb Memorial window by *Ballantyne*; 1896, window in N aisle w of tower by *Kempe*. – PLATE. Parcel-gilt Elizabethan Chalice by *Jons* of Exeter; London-made Paten of 1639; Flagon, 1737; tureen-shaped Almsdish, 1775. – MONUMENTS. Many minor epitaphs, e.g. Elinora Cutcliffe † 1681. – Cap. Richard Brown † 1797, by *Regnart*, large with sarcophagus and big trophy above it.

CHRIST CHURCH, Portland Street, 1844. A grotesque stuccoed two-tower façade. Actually the towers are both part of a s front. Interior well and truly debased. The style is vaguely Italian Medieval.

ST NICHOLAS. Situated, highly picturesquely, on a rock between sea and harbour (cf. below). Small and in the C18 at the latest converted into a lighthouse. Lantern over the w end, sash windows. The entrance now in the E.

ST PETER, Highfield Road. 1902–3, by *Fellowes Prynne* (GR).

ST PHILIP AND ST JAMES. Large, correct and rather dull; 1856, by *Hayward*.

The old centre was the harbour, sheltered behind the greyish-green rock on which stands St Nicholas's Chapel. The PIER was originally built by the Bourchiers, Earls of Bath, rebuilt and enlarged in 1760 and again enlarged in 1824–9. Low Water Jetty added 1873. A picturesque row of small town houses lines the quayside on the N, i.e. towards the sea, and the w. No special buildings worth mentioning except the ROYAL BRITANNIA HOTEL, nice Early Victorian, and emphatically, the MANOR

HOUSE, s of the harbour, a big brick building, three-storeyed, with central bay-window, two windows each side and an additional lower one-window wing each side. No decoration at all, but in character much like the substantial houses of *c*. 1700 along village greens in the home counties. The old town spread in its modest way w of the harbour, up to FORE STREET, where C17 interiors in No. 3 show the pre-Georgian extent. St Philip and St James marks the break between Georgian and Victorian Ilfracombe. To the w of the church the VICTORIA PLEASURE GROUNDS, the PAVILION (*W. H. Gould*, 1888) with iron winter garden and chaste and somewhat joyless façade of 1924. Earlier and more characteristic of Ilfracombe close to the Pavilion the COLLINGWOOD HOTEL, all barge-boarded, i.e. the type of the mid C19 villa, and the former ILFRACOMBE HOTEL of 1867–71 (additions 1892; now Municipal Offices), in multi-coloured bricks, with Gothic windows and French pavilion roof, much like a thoroughly prosperous private mansion. Add to it the RUNNACLEAVE HOTEL, a three- to four-storeyed terrace of rock-faced stone with yellow brick trimmings, pointed windows and gables, and you have a fair cross-section through the somewhat grim styles of High Victorian pleasure architecture.

Much more attractive the remains of the beginnings of Ilfracombe as a resort: the TUNNEL BATHS, 1836, a 46b small one-storeyed stuccoed building with a Greek Doric entrance *in antis*. Nearly opposite BATH PLACE, two houses with a combined Greek Doric entrance, most incorrectly designed. In addition, a few long terraces began to appear about 1835 higher up the hill, in positions similar to those of the slightly earlier terraces of, for example, Torquay: from w to e ADELAIDE TERRACE, with Roman Doric porches, MONTPELIER TERRACE, even more modest (note the names which date the buildings!) and HILLSBOROUGH TERRACE, also with Greek Doric porches. Of wealthier individual houses only a few need attention: CASTLE HOUSE, just sw of Hillsborough Terrace, with a pretty Gothic N front to the sea, and

LASTON HOUSE, a little farther E of Hillsborough Road, with a thatched lodge adorned by a crenellated Gothic turret.

CHAMBERCOMBE FARM, 1 m. SE. Mainly C16–C17, though reputed to date back to 1162.

PREHISTORIC SITES (all within 9 miles).

ARLINGTON BECCOTT. W of the main road from Kentisbury Ford to Arlington Beccott is a 5 ft tall standing stone, down Yea Lane. It marks a bend in an ancient way, and is roughly rectangular.

BENNETTS MOUTH. ½ m. S of Lee Bay, a contorted stone stands in a field 30 yds N of the footpath across fields from Dammage Barton to Bennetts Mouth Cove. It is a markstone, and its upper end is hook-shaped.

CHEGLINCH. ¾ m. SE of Mullacott Cross is a stone, now fallen, in Crook Park field. It marks a right-angled bend in High Cheglinch Lane.

COIL CROSS. ½ m. W of Mattocks Down is a conical markstone on a hill.

GREYSTONE. Above Woolacombe, close to Seymour villas. 7 ft high. The N and E faces show signs of having been dressed square.

HOLVEL. A stone, 2 ft 8 in. high, may have marked the way to the spring from which the neighbouring farm takes its name.

INSTOW

ST JOHN BAPTIST. S transept and chancel probably the oldest parts. In the chancel windows of c. 1300, but all renewed (the same design as at Westleigh nearby). The N aisle with straightheaded three-light windows (each light with a flat ogee top) is dated 1547 by an inscription on two of the piers of the arcade. It says that Richard Waterman and his wife Emma erected the aisle. The arcade has piers of A type (not of granite) with capitals of B type. Ceiled wagon-roof in the aisle. W tower with diagonal buttresses, tall rectangular NE stair-turret and no pinnacles. – FONT. Plain, Norman, of block-capital shape. – TILES. Of the usual Barnstaple designs, in the chancel. – PLATE. Chalice and Paten by *Jons* of Exeter, probably 1576. – Exceptionally good silver-gilt Hanap by *Terry* of London, 1611. The top is an openwork obelisk, the body has bulbous embossed leaf and flower work. Between body and foot openwork scrolls. – MONUMENT. Humphrey Sibthorp, the celebrated botanist of the *Flora Graeca*, † 1797, and buried with a very Grécian monument at Bath Abbey. At Instow only a nicely executed oval inscription tablet by *Kendall* of Exeter.

By the estuary of the river some nice minor early C19 seaside villas, mostly semi-detached.

LIMEKILN by the estuary, looking very fortress-like.

INWARDLEIGH

CHURCH. Architecturally uninteresting. Low w tower with diagonal buttresses, nave and N aisle (three-bay arcade of granite piers of A type with capitals only to the main shafts and depressed pointed arches). Windows straight-headed. – FONT. Norman of block-capital shape. Shaft and foot with rosette, etc., decoration, the semicircular surfaces of the bowl re-cut probably in the C16. – STAINED GLASS. C14 angels in the tracery of the N aisle E window. – TILES. Of Barnstaple make: a few. – PLATE. Chalice by *Jons* of Exeter, 1575.

JACOBSTOWE

ST JAMES. w tower with diagonal buttresses and pinnacles, aisleless nave. – FONT. Square with chamfered angles; featureless. – MONUMENT. Lady Ellen Astley † 1849, epitaph by *Ternouth* of Pimlico, London, with two large allegorical females.

BROOMFIELD MANOR: *see* p. 63.
DOCKPORT: *see* p. 80.

KENNERLEIGH

ST JOHN BAPTIST. Small. Very restored. Oblong unbuttressed w tower with small pyramid-covered pinnacles and C19 pyramid roof. Low nave and one aisle, the four-bay arcade with piers of type A section with capitals only to the main shafts. Old ceiled wagon-roof of chancel. – SCREEN. Small fragments of cornice used in the partition walls of the vestry.

KENTISBURY

ST THOMAS. N aisle and chancel, 1875; the rest old. W tower tall, with buttresses of type B, a NE stair-turret, and no pinnacles. S porch with decorated capitals, one of the handsome SUN DIALS by *Berry* above the doorway, and a wagon-roof with bosses. – SCREEN. Bits of Perp standard type A tracery used in the tower screen. – PLATE. Elizabethan Chalice and Paten by *Mathew* of Barnstaple; plain Paten on stand, 1685.

BARTON. Close to the church, with three-light mullioned windows and a date-stone 1674.

KENTISBURY DOWN, $1\frac{1}{2}$ m. E. Roughly circular hill, with a spur on the N. On this four standing stones and some other prehistoric remains.

KINGS NYMPTON

ST JAMES. Low, unbuttressed W tower with very small openings and recently renewed spire, the tower arch pointed and unmoulded. Nave, N transept (an early medieval tradition) also with pointed and unmoulded arch towards the nave, and S aisle. The aisle is embattled and open to the nave by a tall five-bay arcade with piers of A type and capitals only to the main shafts. A coffin-shaped doorway and door in the chancel N wall. S porch with cross-ribbed unceiled wagon-roof. Wagon-roofs in the church as well. CEILURE, i.e. specially decorated wagon-roof, panelled and with cross-ribs, above the rood screen. In the chancel the roof was plastered early in the C19 to paint a picture on it of sky, clouds and a large cross. – REREDOS, early C18, big, with Ionic pilasters. The COMMUNION RAILS with alternating twisted balusters and columns also early C18. The FONT (baluster shaft and fluted bowl) probably of the same date. Jacobean PANELLING in the S aisle E (Pollard) chapel. – SCREEN.

Complete with ribbed coving and cornice (three bands of ornament). The tracery type A standard, the panels between the ribs of the coving have, in the nave tracery, in the aisle leaf, head, etc., motifs. – PLATE. On loan at the Victoria and Albert Museum, London.

KINGS NYMPTON PARK. Fine Early Georgian mansion of the Buller family. Moderate size, brick with stone dressings, s windows wide, the main front with a centre of four Ionic giant pilasters on a rusticated ground floor, carrying a decorated pediment. The entrance porch on the opposite side c. 1845. Inside, low hall with four columns to divide it into three aisles. Several pretty fireplaces of c. 1740–50.

KNIGHTSHAYES COURT NR TIVERTON

By *William Burges*, 1870–3. Red sandstone with yellow stone dressings. Symmetrical Tudor s front, the other sides asymmetrical and more interesting, with *Burges's* ham-fisted, but robust detail: ample plate tracery, some occasional circular turrets, lancet windows, etc. The interior meant to be sumptuously decorated (original drawings at the house). Much of this decoration was never carried out, other parts have been removed. The hall with timber roof remains, and one other room.

KNOWSTONE

ST PETER. W tower with diagonal buttresses and polygonal NE stair-turret; no pinnacles. Most windows straight-headed. The interest of the church is its plain Norman s door and the odd three-bay arcade between nave and N aisle: unmoulded roundheaded arches on square piers with three-part abaci instead of capitals. – PULPIT. One panel of a former screen is used. – PLATE. Transferred from Molland; Chalice of 1664; Paten of 1695; Flagon of 1700. – MONUMENT. John Culme † 1691, epitaph with two figures resting on the broken pediment.

(SHAPCOTT BARTON, 2 m. E. Manor house of the C16 with older parts. Hall with door and screens Elizabethan. *Hoskins*.)

LANDCROSS

HOLY TRINITY. Aisleless little chapel with projecting
slate-hung bell-turret (of after 1809). Ceiled wagon-roof
inside. – FONT. Norman, of block-capital shape, with bits
of decoration only at the foot. – PULPIT with Early
Renaissance panels similar to those usual on bench-ends.
– BENCH-ENDS. Some with shields, profile heads, and
Perp leaves, but two with tumblers in characteristically
Elizabethan little arcades. – PLATE. Cup on short stem by
Jons of Exeter, 1576.

LANDKEY

ST PAUL. A stately church. W tower with type-B buttresses,
polygonal NE stair-turret higher than the tower battlements, gargoyles below the battlements, and no pinnacles.
Nave and N aisle, N and S transepts, both embattled
and with gargoyles, S porch attached to the S transept
and provided with fleuron-decorated outer and inner
doorways. Evidence of the pre-Perp church is the chancel
with a small lancet window on the N side and the inner
arch mouldings of the windows on the E and S sides.
Squint from the S transept into the chancel. The arcade
between nave and N aisle is Perp, three bays with slender
piers of B section, but capitals only to the main shafts.
Also Perp the arches to the S and N transept. Ceiled
wagon-roofs in nave, aisle and S porch; the beams of the
nave roof rest on head-corbels. (Head-corbels also as stops
of hood-moulds of windows; the Perp mason at Landkey
must have been specially fond of figure sculpture.) –
FONT. Octagonal, Perp, with tracery panels on the shaft,
quatrefoil decoration on the bowl. – PLATE. Elizabethan
Chalice and Paten by *Mathew* of Barnstaple; Flagon and
Paten of 1715–16. – MONUMENTS. Cross-legged knight
and lady wearing wimple, *c.* 1300; must originally have
been of fine quality. The knight has the upper part of his
body turned so that his cheek lies on the pillow, no doubt
to look at his slim young wife. – C14 effigy of a lady,
stiffer than the earlier couple. – Sir Arthur Acland † 1610

35

and wife: big standing wall monument. Lady Acland recumbent, Sir Arthur behind her and a little higher up, semi-reclining. To her head and feet smaller kneeling figures. Simple decoration of the back wall. The figure sculpture of good quality.

LANGTREE

CHURCH. The W tower has its stair-turret (reaching above the battlements of tower) in the middle of the S side (a feature not unusual in S Devon, but very exceptional in this part of the county). Buttresses only at the foot, no pinnacles. Wide nave, N aisle with arcade of 4 + 2 bays, the piers of granite, type A, with capitals only to the main shafts, and depressed arches. The N windows straight-headed, the chancel E window of a rare Perp tracery design. – FONT. Octagonal, Perp, with simple patterns in the panels. – PULPIT. Late C17 with carved garlands, cherubs' heads, etc. – Two CHAIRS in the chancel with re-used Flemish C16 reliefs of Christ carrying the Cross and Christ crucified. – ROYAL ARMS. Large, of plaster, with strapwork decoration, very much as usual in N Cornwall.

LAPFORD

ST THOMAS OF CANTERBURY. W tower with diagonal buttresses, polygonal stair-turret at the SE angle (unusual), no pinnacles. Low in the S side recess for an image (cf. South and North Molton). Nave and N aisle, separated by a rather tall granite arcade (piers of A type but with standard Devon leaf capitals), unceiled N aisle wagon-roof, splendid CEILURE with cross-ribs and *roses en-soleil* above the ROOD SCREEN. The latter the best in the neighbour- 22 hood, with type-B tracery, ribbed coving with Renaissance detail between the ribs, and a very complete cornice with four strips of decoration and cresting. In type similar to Atherington. The PARCLOSE SCREEN simpler. – S DOOR supposed to be Norman; in a Norman doorway. The door knocker looks old enough, but can hardly be dated accurately. – BENCH-ENDS. Numerous, with initials, 28b monograms (St John family), profile heads, Renaissance and Late Flamboyant ornament; also figure with scourge (cf. Down St Mary), and heart, feet, and hands to symbolize Christ's Passion.

(BURY BARTON, 1 m. s. According to Mr G. W. Copeland the private chapel of the manor house, a detached structure, survives.)

LEE

Picturesque village down a combe to the sea. A few nice houses by the beach (date 1627 on THE SMUGGLERS). Higher up THREE OLD MAIDS COTTAGE, 1653: show cottage, white and thatched; the prototype of so much that was artificially made 'orné' about 1800, but perhaps itself improved in looks at that time.

PREHISTORIC STONES. 1 m. ESE, WHITESTONE (N of the road between Pludd and Lincombe), a boulder of veined quartz, 9 ft high and 21 ft in circumference. – Near the fifteenth hole of the Lee Bay Golf Links a triangular standing stone, 4 ft high and diamond-shaped.

LEE ABBEY see LYNTON

LITTLEHAM

ST SWITHIN. Early plan preserved on the N side with transept and also two lancet windows. W tower with big buttresses covering the angles and no pinnacles. Perp s aisle with low arcade (piers of A type, not of granite, and capitals of Devon standard). – FONT. Perp, granite, coarse. – BENCH-ENDS with unusually bold, broad Early Renaissance scrolls. – STAINED GLASS by *Kempe*. – PAINTING. Saintly Bishop, *c*. 1300, in N transept; badly preserved. – PLATE. Pre-Reformation Chalice, presented in 1889, probably foreign. Hexagonal stem, large knot of six lozenges with the letters SAPRIA; Chalice and Paten by *Jons* of Exeter, 1576; Paten by *J. Chadwick*, 1696. – MONUMENT. Lt.-Gen. H. H. Crealock † 1891 by *Temple Moore* (who also designed the rood screen on the pattern of that of Patricio in Monmouthshire). The memorial is a recumbent figure with angels on a super-Gothic big and tall tomb-chest.

LITTLE TOMS HILL see EXMOOR

LITTLE TORRINGTON

St Giles. Roughcast narrow w tower with thin diagonal buttresses and pinnacles. Nave and s aisle, the arcade of four bays with granite piers of A type with capitals only to the main shafts, elementarily decorated abaci and depressed pointed arches. – FONT. Circular, very primitive, with projected ribbed corners; what date? Jacobean cover. – PLATE. Chalice of 1573; Cup on baluster stem by *IK*, dated 1600. – MONUMENTS. Henry Stevens of Cross † 1802, by *Rouw* of London, large epitaph with mourning female bent over an urn. – Sarah Fortescue † 1821, single, by *Baily*.

CROSS: *see* p. 79.

LONGSTONE see EXMOOR

LOXBEARE

CHURCH. Tiny with an unbuttressed N tower stump, nave and lower chancel. s door Norman with outer zigzag moulding of jambs and arch. – PULPIT. With sounding board; simple, probably *c.* 1660. – COMMUNION RAIL. Jacobean balusters, perhaps re-used. – WEST GALLERY. Jacobean; fragments re-used in the chancel seats. – The BELLS (not usually mentioned in these volumes) are of special interest here: three by *J.T.*, a C15 Exeter bell founder. The *Little Guide* calls the bell chamber 'a perfect example of the medieval period'. – MONUMENTS to members of the Cudmore family; minor.

LOXHORE

St Michael. Chancel with two small s lancet windows and an E window, unusually narrow (only two lights) but with a transome. w tower with diagonal buttresses and no pinnacles. N aisle of three bays divided from the nave by wooden piers with no arches, but a straight entablature. The section of the piers quite exceptional. The church had originally a tympanum between nave and chancel (cf. Molland, Parracombe). – FONT COVER. C16, concave outline, crocketed top, still no Elizabethan features. – PEWS. Nice, plain, stained black. – PLATE. Nice graceful Early Elizabethan Chalice with Paten, marked *P.Q.*, probably by *Quick* of Barnstaple. – MONUMENTS. Long, small, slate inscription plate to Richard Carpenter † 1627, with lettering in many different types. – Epitaphs to Edward and Philip Hammond † 1653 and 1704.

LUFFINCOTT

ST JAMES. Finely placed with a view towards the wooded slopes of the river Tamar. The W tower rebuilt 1791. This is testified by an inscription. If it were not, the style would not show it. Old materials must have been re-used. Unbuttressed, with obelisk pinnacles. What, however, is disarmingly 1791, is the sash-windows put in on the N side of the nave. The nave has a nice boarded wagon-roof. – FONT. Granite, octagonal, badly preserved. – PLATE. Small Cup on baluster stem, 1635; Almsdish or Sweetmeat Dish, 1663.

LUNDY

The island lies 12 m. NNW of Hartland Point. It is about 3 m. long and half a mile wide, a precipitous rock with only one safe anchoring place on the E side close to the S tip. It has been inhabited from early days. N of the Three-quart Wall a hut-circle, and E of Shuttle Point a Kistvaen have been found. In the old burial ground (by the Old Light) also a Romano-British inscribed stone can be seen. The inscription commemorates a Tigernus son of Tigernus. From the middle of the C12 to 1321 the de Marisco family were masters of Lundy, more than once in open opposition to the kings. Then and later the island was frequently used as a base for piratical expeditions into the Bristol Channel. The final flourish of this lawless existence was the time about the middle of the C18, when Lundy was leased to Thomas Benson M.P., a Bideford merchant and slave-owner as well as smuggler. In 1836 William Hudson Heaven bought

Lundy. Under the dynasty of the Heavens many improve-
ments were made. Since 1925 Mr M. Coles Harman has
been the proprietor of Lundy. The island is visited mostly
because of its flora and fauna, especially its seabirds. Architecturally it has little to give.

MARISCO CASTLE, s of the hotel. Scanty remains of moat
and outer walls. The Keep rectangular with a two-stepped
centre projection to the E. Inside the Keep ruins of C18
cottages.

ST HELEN, 1896, by *J. Norton*. The furnishings mainly by
the indefatigable *Hems* of Exeter. The ancient church is
now completely in ruins. It lies inside the Old Burial
Ground. Only fragments of walls just above ground.

OLD LIGHT. The lighthouse was built by Trinity House in
1819. It is a beautifully proportioned granite structure 90
ft high. It was replaced in 1897 by the new North and
South Lights.

MANOR FARM HOTEL. Parts of various dates, the oldest
the centre, then the N range.

MILLCOMBE. The house of the owner, built in a perfectly
sheltered position by W. H. Heaven, shortly after he had
bought the island, and surrounded by a garden with
shrubs and trees, the only place where Lundy can be seen
in so gentle a mood.

ST JOHN BAPTIST, 1871, by *E. Dolly* (GR); enlarged 1908.

LYNMOUTH

The chief attraction is, of course, scenic. Architecturally the
QUAY has on the W a pretty terrace of climbing-up cottages, called MARS HILL. Surrounding the harbour
there are a few small Early Victorian houses with Gothic
detail and some barge-boarded villas, as they are so
characteristic of *c*. 1840–60. Amongst the latter some
were built as hotels. Shelley had a cottage at Lynmouth
as early as 1812, and Southey wrote enthusiastically about
the village which, he said, was the finest spot he ever saw,
except for Cintra and the Arrabida. Amongst the pre-
Victorian houses are two facing a lush lawn right down by
the stony harbour: ROCK HOUSE with a thatched

verandah on tree trunks and a mildly Gothic front,
and the MANOR HOUSE, plain and square (with additions). Above Lynmouth on the E the TORS HOTEL, a
characteristic example of how the barge-boarded villa
was later, in Lynmouth's heyday, enlarged by grossly
half-timbered gables, etc.

The most popular feature of Lynmouth is the RHENISH
TOWER, built about 1860 by one General Rawdon to
store salt water for indoor baths. The tower is small and
none too Rhenish-looking. But the allusion to Germany
is appropriate. For the popularity of Lynmouth and its
environs coincides with that of journeys up the Rhine to
the Black Forest. The *Zahnradbahn* up to Lynton, the
tidy footpaths through the woods, the frequency of
conifers, all gives a decidedly German flavour.

LYNTON

ST MARY. Unbuttressed, unpinnacled tower at the SW end.
S wall of the nave, 1741. New chancel in the E.E. style by
Dalby, 1868–9, re-used as E end to the N aisle, in con-
junction with larger scale rebuilding of 1893–1905. In
1893–4 *Sedding* built a new broad nave with wagon-roof
and broad fine Dec W window and N and S aisles with
octagonal arcade piers. Later still, in 1905, *H. Wilson*
Sedding's pupil, built a new chancel, oddly enough in the
Romanesque style; not one of his best designs. – FONT
Octagonal, with two shallow blank roundheaded arches on
each side. Elizabethan cover. – GLASS. N and S windows
nicely ornamented in the Art Nouveau taste. – PLATE
Flagon by *Boutell*, 1724, and other C18 pieces. – MONU-
MENT. Thomas Grose † 1734, painted by *Phelps* of
Porlock.

HOLY SAVIOUR, Roman Catholic Church and Convent
1910, by *Leonard Stokes*. The church with a plain gabled
façade and an Italian-looking bellcote by the side of a
gable. Very odd Neo-Perp windows. Interior white and
Italian, tunnel-vaulted. W gallery on two Ionic columns
Choir raised and with *cancelli* of coloured marbles. The
convent decently and honestly utilitarian.

METHODIST CHURCH. 1910, by *Latrobe & Weston*, with fanciful Art Nouveau stone front.

TOWN HALL. 1898–1900, by *Read & Macdonald*. Small, but certainly an attempt at municipal architecture in a holiday spirit. Rough and dressed stone, wooden balconies, two short castellated turrets and gaily half-timbered gables. Utterly un-Devonian.

Lynton was no more than a hamlet before Queen Victoria's time. The railway reached it only in 1898 and has since deserted it again. A nice example of the early architecture is the ROYAL CASTLE HOTEL, built as a private house in 1810, in a glorious position high above and overlooking the sea. Similar modest long white houses in various places. The hotel style is High to Late Victorian, i.e. from the grimness of some of Ilfracombe and Westward Ho! to the heavy-handed gaiety of fancy tile-hanging and turrets and gables with woodwork painted white (VALLEY OF ROCKS HOTEL, N side, by *R. Plumbe*, 1888).

LEE ABBEY. 1850, on the site of a farmhouse supposed to represent the manor house of the Wichehalse family. Sumptuous, ham-fisted Gothic, with Tudor living-quarters, a big octagonal chapter-house-like library (odd fancy tracery in the large windows, timber ribs and a timber pendant), and in the outbuildings attempts at buttressed monastic walls, a monastic gatehouse, etc. Also an isolated ecclesiastical-looking tower on a hill close to the sea: 'Lee was never the site of a monastic foundation. It is only a melodramatic abbey' (*Murray's Guidebook*, 1872).

GLENTHORNE. Built by the Rev. W. S. Halliday about 1830, in a wonderfully sheltered cove far below the Lynton–Porlock road and reached on a private road with serpentines as daring as in the Alps. The house was designed by *Mr Halliday* himself in an undistinguished Neo-Tudor style.

PREHISTORIC SITES. s of, and under, CASTLE ROCK, for instance, a Pound, 40 ft in diameter. – In the VALLEY OF ROCKS a collection of stones, possibly representing the remains of hut-circles.

OLD BURROW CASTLE, 4 m. E. The remains of a late C4
Roman signal station, built on the coast to give warning of
the approach of raiding ships from Ireland and the North.
It stands 1,100 ft above sea level. From the site a good
view may be obtained over the Bristol Channel, over
Exmoor, the Great Hangman, Yenworthy, and Porlock
Bay. The outer earthwork has a diameter of 285 ft. The
ditch outside is 3–6 ft deep. The external diameter of the
ditch is 322 ft. There are two gaps in the earthwork, on
the N and SW, that on the N being modern. In the middle
of the centre area is a square enclosure, in the middle of which a small mound, 10 ft in diameter and 15 in.
high.

ROBOROUGH CASTLE. SE of Lynton on the ridge between
Fursehill and Hoar Watters, just above Lyncombe Wood.
Circular, 83 yd diameter. W side best condition. Ditch
8 ft 1 in. deep and rampart 12 ft. Single fosse and rampart.

STOCK CASTLE. SE of Lynton on the W slope of the same
ridge. Approximately square, with rounded corners, 58 yd
in diameter. Single fosse and rampart; fosse ploughed
away, rampart 8 ft 10 in. at highest point.

MADDOCKS DOWN see EXMOOR

MARIANSLEIGH

ST MARY. Gutted by fire in 1932. In connexion with the
fire some interesting remains of a C13 church in the S side
of the nave were discovered consisting of two arches with
circular piers of a former S aisle. W tower with buttresses
only at the foot. The tower arch narrow and low, completely unmoulded. N aisle Perp, the piers of B type with
standard capitals, the windows straightheaded.

MARISCO CASTLE see LUNDY

MARTINHOE

ST MARTIN. Small unbuttressed, unpinnacled W tower,
narrower than the nave. Low, depressed, pointed opening

of the tower to the nave: a very primitive form (cf. Parracombe). Nave and lower chancel. The chancel *c.* 1300 (E window Victorian). N aisle and N arcade 1866. Gorgeous stiff-leaf decorated FONT of 1864. – SCREEN. Very little of the tracery of the wainscoting is all that remains. – PLATE. Chalice of wine-glass shape, 1640; Paten, 1784. CHURCH HOUSE. SE of the church.

MARWOOD

ST MICHAEL. The position is attractive. The tall w tower points out of the village across green hills and woods, the E end faces a pretty Late Georgian house. W tower with buttresses only at the foot, and no pinnacles. Embattled S porch. The S transept is older, of the C13 (*see* the single lancet on the E side and the unmoulded pointed arch to the nave). The chancel also is C13, though remodelled in the C14 (E window tracery C19). The S door by its moulding and small corbels must also be C14. The N aisle is Late Perp with straightheaded windows and the usual Devon arcade (five bays) with B-type piers and standard leaf capitals. Unceiled wagon-roofs. The chief interest of the church is its SCREEN. Only the aisle sections preserved. It has standard type-A tracery, but unusual wainscoting, with panels full of Early Renaissance decoration, complete ribbed coving with Early Renaissance motifs between the ribs, just as at Atherington. Also as at Atherington the fact that the coving at the back has only tracery between the ribs. The back of the rood loft is preserved, a rarity. It has rude, broad, elementary Perp motifs. On the wainscoting panels of the door is recorded the donation of the screen by a parson of Marwood called Beauple. In guidebooks it is implied that that dates the screen 1520. However, all that is known is that Beauple was rector in 1520, but no other name or date appears in records between 1520 and 1561. So the screen may well be as late as 1535 or 1540, which is more likely. – BENCH-ENDS. Of Devon–Cornwall type and with the usual initials, shields, etc.; also a few figures of saints. – ROYAL ARMS. Big, plaster, time of George III. – SUN DIAL. By

John Berry, 1762 (cf. Tawstock). – PLATE. Elizabethan Chalice by *Mathew* of Barnstaple; Paten, 1698; Almsdish, 1678.

(WESTCOTT BARTON. According to Dr Hoskins good example of a barton arranged round an inner courtyard.)

MEETH

ST MICHAEL. Plain Norman S doorway with only the smallest amount of decoration in the outer moulding of the arch. Norman windows also in the N side of the nave and the rectangular NE stair-turret of the unbuttressed W tower. The absence of a W door also is usually evidence of an early date. The tower arch towards the nave is pointed but unmoulded. – FONT. Norman, square on five shafts, undecorated. – ROYAL ARMS. Uncommonly swagger; dated 1704. Could they be by *John Abbot* (*see* Frithelstock)? – PLATE. Chalice on baluster stem, London-made, 1642. – MONUMENT. Prudence Lamb † 1843, by *Ternout* of Pimlico; epitaph with angel carrying the young woman up to heaven.

MERTON

ALL SAINTS. W tower with buttresses leaving the angles free, obelisk pinnacles. Nave and N aisle, the five-bay arcade with piers of A type (capitals only to the main shafts), primitively decorated abaci and depressed pointed arches. S transept with S recess for a not preserved monument. – FONT. Square, Norman, the under edge with three scallops to each side; Jacobean cover. – STAINED GLASS. E window by *Kempe*, 1898. – PLATE. Wine Cup on trumpet stem and Cover with decoration of birds and trees, inscribed 1688. Same marks on a Sweetmeat Dish on trumpet stem.

MESHAW

ST JOHN BAPTIST. 1838, by *R. D. Gould*, except for the W tower of 1691. – PLATE. Set of 1693. – MONUMENT. James Courtenay † 1685.

MILTON DAMEREL

HOLY TRINITY. W tower rebuilt with the old materials in
1892: small, slim, narrower than the nave, without
buttresses, W door, and pinnacles, i.e. early medieval. The
chancel followed about 1300–1330; *see* the tracery of
the windows: S window still geometrical (cinquefoils),
though with pointed trefoil lights (cf. the piscina), but
E window with ogee reticulation. The N aisle and the nave
S windows latest Perp (straightheaded, no tracery). Inside
an unusually wide nave, but the usual arcade (3 + 2 bays)
with A-type piers, rudely decorated capitals and depressed
arches. – PULPIT. Rustic late C17 work. – ROYAL ARMS.
Plaster 1664, very much like in North Cornwall churches.
– TILES. In nave and aisle, of the usual Barnstaple type. –
PLATE. Chalice and Paten by *Jons* of Exeter, 1577; Paten,
1705.

MODBURY *see* BUCKLAND FILLEIGH

MOLLAND

ST MARY. Exterior of no special interest (W tower with
diagonal buttresses and no pinnacles; polygonal NE stair-
turret). But one of the memorable church interiors of
Devon, very completely preserved in a pre-Victorian
form. Small, with N aisle (Perp three-bay arcade of B-
type piers with standard capitals and depressed arches*),
and N chancel chapel. Old wagon-roofs. Nave and aisle
with BOX PEWS, the PULPIT of the three-decker type
with trumpeting angel on the sounding board, the
SCREEN carries a solid 'tympanum' with the Royal Arms
and Ten Commandments painted in 1808, the COMMUN-
ION RAILS *c.* 1700. – FONT. Norman, square, scalloped
under edge. – MONUMENTS. Fragments of Late Perp
tomb-chest with quatrefoil decoration. – David Barry †
1664, John Courtenay † 1666, John Courtenay † 1693,
John Courtenay † 1732: all rather unimportant epitaphs.
WEST MOLLAND, I m. W. House of the Courtenays, the
front Georgianized, the back still with Tudor features.

* Low against one pier a niche with a broken image of a saint.

MOLTON, SOUTH, see SOUTH MOLTON
MOLTON, NORTH, see NORTH MOLTON

MONKLEIGH

St George. All Perp. w tower with buttresses of B type and pinnacles; all windows Perp, some on the s side of the same unusual design as at Weare Giffard nearby. Arcade to the s aisle of five bays with granite piers of A type with capitals only to the main shafts, decorated abaci and depressed pointed arches. Ceiled wagon-roof in the aisle. The most important part of the church is the SE chapel, or ANNERY CHAPEL, with the monument to Sir William Hankford † 1422, Chief Justice of the King's Bench. The tomb-chest is placed in a recess with a depressed pointed arch, exceptionally finely cusped and with an exceptionally finely carved cresting. The tomb-chest is decorated with seven pinnacled, ogee-arched niches, the centre one higher than the others. There is no effigy on the lid. The SCREEN between aisle and chapel also amongst the most remarkable of the many Devon screens. Its tracery is of the standard A type, but the carving in the spandrels, especially on the E side, is superb. Mostly leaves, but there is also a pelican. The date probably the same as the hall screen at Weare Giffard with very similar spandrels (or are they at Weare Giffard imported from the missing parts of the Monkleigh screen?). – BENCH-ENDS in the Annery Chapel a jumble of the usual Devon type of panels and Elizabethan bits. – FONT. Norman, circular, of a very uncommon design. The bowl is fluted, and at the top of the shaft there is also fluting, pleated outward and then again inward, a little like a Chinese lantern. – COMMUNION RAILS. C17. – STAINED GLASS. Many bits in the E window of the s aisle. – MONUMENTS. Brass on the N wall of the chancel, placed in a patchwork of bits from some C16 monument, tops of twisted columns, carrying the springings of little vaults, etc. – Two little slate plates, one to Henry Hurding † 1627 and family, the other to Jane Coffin † 1646, and wife, a reclining figure. – Epitaph to William Gaye † 1631, with two frontal demi-

30b

figures in niches, both with cheek leaning against hand.
Below, it says:

> Since Epitaphs have given speech to stones
> Their rhetorick extorted Sighs, Tears, Groans.
> Some teach divinitye, but this commends
> Drys tears, stops sighs, and strangleth groans of
> friends—

because of William Gaye's 'temp'rance, prudence, can-
dour, pietye'.

MONK OKEHAMPTON

ALL SAINTS. The low, unbuttressed w tower with big pinnacles is the only medieval part of the church. The rest
1855 (by *Harper & Arnold*: GR). The E window was exhibited at the Crystal Palace in 1851. – PLATE. Paten,
Saucer, and Sweetmeat Dish, decorated with punched
work, by *Nightingale*, London, 1655.
ASH HOUSE: see p. 41.

MORCHARD BISHOP

ST MARY. High up with a dominating w tower 95 ft high;
type-B buttresses, short pinnacles, polygonal NE stair-
turret. w window of four lights in the style of Exeter
Cathedral. N and s aisles, both embattled. Chancel C18
with roundheaded windows, panelling inside, below of
timber, above of stucco. Fine C18 REREDOS with Corinthian pilasters. The PULPIT made up from the reader's
desk, panelling as in the chancel. The COMMUNION
RAIL earlier than the C18. The arcades between nave and
aisles of three bays, the piers and arches of red sandstone
(piers of B type with capitals only to the main shafts). The
4th bay opens from the chancel into the chancel chapels.
Piers of limestone, the arch on the s side with Perp
panelling. The chapel here probably the family chapel of
the Eyston family. The tomb recess with the MONUMENT
of two recumbent figures: husband in civilian clothes and
wife, early C16. The carving must originally have been of
respectable quality. – SCREEN. Reconstructed recently

from original parts which indicate tracery of B type and ribbed coving with Renaissance detail between the ribs as at Lapford.

MOREBATH

St George. Lower parts of w tower unbuttressed, probably C13. Nave and N aisle Perp. Arcade of A type with capitals only to the four main shafts of the piers. Wagon-roof in the aisle. – PLATE. Exeter-type Chalice and Paten, 1593; Paten on stand, 1698. – MONUMENTS. Minor Late Georgian epitaphs.

MORETON
½ m. w of Bideford

The house is of 1824, eight bays wide, two and a half storeys high, with hipped roof and a one-storey, four-column porch. In the same style on the same estate HIGHER WINSFORD.

MORTEHOE

St Mary Magdalene. In an exquisite position close to Morte Point. The oldest part of the church is the tower on the N side connected to the church by a low roundheaded doorway. The tower is unbuttressed and unpinnacled. Its N door, presumably originally the entry into a N porch, is pointed and rudely built of large stones. The church is supposed to have been founded by Sir William de Tracey in 1170. C13 enlargements comprise the chancel with two lancet windows and an unmoulded chancel arch on plain imposts, perhaps the nave walls (plain roundheaded s door) and the s transept. Perp addition the N aisle of two bays, E of the tower, with rough octagonal piers, no capitals, and two-centred chamfered arches. A more surprising addition is the arcade of one and a half bays between nave and s transept. One slender octagonal pier dated 1618 stands in line with the w wall of the transept, but behind it a diagonal connexion has been created between that wall and the nave s wall. It is vaulted and has two (new) two-light windows. What was its purpose, and

what is its date? Ceiled wagon-roof in the s transept, open
in the nave. – BENCH-ENDS. Forty-eight of the usual
Devon type and designs, Instruments of the Passion,
saints, coats of arms, many initials, profile heads in
roundels. – MOSAIC. On the chancel arch, large figures,
in the Preraphaelite tradition, oddly incongruous in their
place; 1903, by *Selwyn Image*. – ALTAR FRONTALS.
Embroidered, also to *Image*'s designs (shortly before
1903). – STAINED GLASS mostly by *Beer* of Exeter. –
MONUMENT. Tomb-chest in the s transept, probably to
William de Tracey who founded the chantry of St Mary
Magdalene in 1308 and died in 1322. Incised figure of
priest with chalice on the lid. The sides of the tomb show
the Crucifixion, two saints, and otherwise only tracery, but
tracery of considerable historical importance in so far as it
can here be dated safely. That should help in the dating of
much window tracery. The designs are of two- and three-
light blank arches, the lights cusped and pointed, and
besides cinquefoiled circles, pointed quatrefoils, and also
ogee reticulation.

DAMMAGE BARTON, 1 m. E of Mortehoe. Very picturesque grey stone farmhouse, windows and chimneys
C17, but remains of an earlier structure incorporated.
1656 date-stone on a stable building. Barn with semicircular addition.

NEWPORT *see* BARNSTAPLE

NEWTON ST PETROCK

ST PETROCK. The oldest part no doubt the W tower, unbuttressed, with a W door, and with an unmoulded
pointed arch towards the nave. The rest all Perp, N as
well as s windows (chancel 1887) and the arcade between
nave and s aisle (four bays with granite piers of A type,
capitals only to the main shafts and depressed pointed
arches). – FONT. Norman, shapeless big circular bowl on
short shaft. – PULPIT. C19 but with old panels of the
Instruments of the Passion. – BENCH-ENDS. A large
coherent set, with initials, coat of arms, Renaissance

scrolls, etc. – ALTAR TABLE. Elizabethan. – PLATE. A set of 1778–80.

NEWTON TRACEY

ST THOMAS OF CANTERBURY. Aisleless church with several C13 windows preserved. W tower unbuttressed and unpinnacled, the arch towards the nave roundheaded and unmoulded. N aisle C19. – FONT. C13 with elaborate stiff-leaf decoration and cable moulding at the waist. – PLATE. Flat cup-shaped Chalice with trumpet-stem, later C17; Paten by *R. Neale* of London, 1663.

NORTHAM

ST MARGARET. A big church. Tall W tower with diagonal buttresses and pinnacles, polygonal stair-turret on the S side near the E angle. W door with fleurons. W aisle, S transept. Wide nave with wagon-roof on angels, wagon-roofs also in the transept. In the nave, apart from the usual foliage bosses, some with those symbols of the Passion which usually appear on bench-ends. The N aisle was added as late as 1593, as marked on one of the piers. (This yele was made anno 1593): five bays, octagonal piers with raw capitals and double-chamfered arches. – FONT. C13, octagonal with the flat blank arches of the table-top type (but pointed). – MONUMENTS. Several late C18–early C19 epitaphs by such artists as *Kendall* of Exeter, *Gould* of Barnstaple, and *Johnson* of New Road, London. – Sir Charles Chalmers † 1834 and wife † 1840, oval inscription plate with lovely scrolly blackletter script.

NORTHLEW

ST THOMAS OF LEW. A small, but aisled church with some interesting remains of the Norman period, namely, the lower parts of the unbuttressed W tower (windows on S and N sides), the W doorway with one order of colonnettes and a pointed arch, and the low inner tower arch, also pointed. The rest Perp: the pinnacles of the tower, the aisles with their four-bay granite arcades (piers of A-type with capitals only to the main shafts and de-

pressed pointed arches) and their windows (s side four
lights and Perp tracery, set into a wall of ashlared granite;
N side straightheaded without tracery) and the unceiled
wagon-roofs. In the s aisle and the N chancel chapel the
roof has angels against the wallplate; in the N chancel
chapel in addition outstandingly exuberant bosses spreading out big leaves in four directions. – SCREEN. Mostly
new, only the wainscoting original. – BENCH-ENDS. One
of the set dated 1537. The date is interesting, as there is no
Renaissance ornament anywhere, only tracery (some with
Flamboyant forms), initials on shields, and the like. –
PLATE. Elizabethan Chalice and Paten by *Jons* of Exeter

NORTH MOLTON

ALL SAINTS. Tall three-stage tower with type-B buttresses,
a niche with a (bad, though original) figure of the Virgin
on the s side, battlements decorated with quatrefoils, and
tall pinnacles. Three-light aisle windows, and a three-
light E window with an ornamented transome. The five-
bay arcades inside between nave and aisles have piers of A
type with capitals only to the four main shafts. Above the
arcade the un-Devonian motif of a clerestory. Its windows are low, of two lights, with decorated spandrels. –
FONT. Octagonal, Perp, with small figures against the
shaft, and pointed quatrefoils and panelling against the
shallow bowl. – PULPIT. Timber, but otherwise of
exactly the same type as South Molton. The sounding
board is of *c.* 1700. It has a trumpeting angel on the top. –
SCREENS. Rood Screen, Perp, of standard A design, all
across nave and aisles. The two Parclose Screens differ in
design: one has sixteen narrowly set, ungrouped lights
with tall crocketed ogee tops, the other three panels of
four lights each. – CHANCEL PANELLING. 'Jacobean',
though probably as late as the middle of the C17.
Obelisks as crowning motifs. The whole quite exceptionally ornate. – STAINED GLASS. E window by *Wailes*,
1858 (TK). – PLATE. Unusually fine Elizabethan Chalice
and Paten, marked *T.C.* It has a band with odd animals
and leaf decoration on the base. The paten has animals

too. – MONUMENTS. Sir Amyas Bamfylde † 1626, big standing wall-monument of alabaster. Sir Amyas recumbent, his wife seated at his feet, with her hand against her cheek, kneeling figures against tomb-chest and back, the whole flanked by columns and crowned by an open segmental pediment. – John Burgess and George Escott † 1772 and wife, oval epitaph, gracefully done by *King* of Bath.

COURT HOUSE, SW of the church. Built 1553. Long two-storey stone front, the r. side with squareheaded Tudor windows, the porch with an outer Tudor doorway. On the l. side later C17 windows with mullions and transomes. One room has Tudor panelling and a fireplace surround of 1692 (the latter from Poltimore House, South Devon).

COURT HALL, E of the church. Plain two-storey Georgian stone block, seven by five bays.

NORTH PETHERWIN

ST PATERNUS. Its chief architectural features connect the church with Cornwall more than with Devon: N aisle with thick circular Norman piers with many-scalloped capitals. Double-chamfered pointed arches. Clerestory windows (a rarity both in Cornwall and Devon) not above the apexes of the arches below, but above the piers. This oddity appears Norman at St Germans and later at Lostwithiel and Fowey. The style of the small Petherwin clerestory windows (and the aisle windows) is *c.* 1300. The rest of the church Perp. W tower with diagonal buttresses, gargoyles below the battlements, and big cusped pinnacles. S aisle with Perp windows and arcade of five bays with piers of A type and capitals only to the main shafts. The Norman piers are followed on the N side by a chancel chapel of two more bays identical with the arcade. – SCREEN. Only part of the wainscoting of the screen survives. – COMMUNION RAILS. Now under the tower arch, with big balusters and other ornamental motifs which make the initially surprising date 1685 quite convincing. – BENCH-ENDS. Only a few with Instrument of the Passion.

NORTH TAWTON

ST PETER. Much of the outside of granite ashlar. The W tower E.E.: low and unbuttressed. Shingled spire, renovated 1900, nave and two aisles. Arcades of six bays with granite piers of A type with capitals only to the main shafts. The arches are nearly semicircular. No structural division at all between nave and chancel. – Unceiled wagon-roofs to nave and aisles. – BENCH-ENDS. Some in the nave (one with angels holding the arms of the Champernowne family), others re-used behind the altar (tracery panels with pretty roses in leaves in the spandrels). – STAINED GLASS. Angels with shields in the tracery of one N window.

The town of no special beauty. In the SQUARE the former TOWN HALL, now Cinema, of 1849. On the opposite side BROAD HALL, dated 1680, but incorporating the 39a remains of a remarkable C15 private house: doorway and bay-window of six lights, the mullions, as far as not replaced, finely carved with Perp foliage. Nothing of its history seems to be known.

COTTLES BARTON: see p. 78.

BURTON HALL. Mid-Victorian villa to the N of the town, weatherboarded walls and timber trim, very Victorian, yet curiously outlandish in detail, the explanation being that the building was brought over from Norway.

NUTCOMBE see CLAYHANGER

NYMET ROWLAND

ST BARTHOLOMEW. Small church with Norman S door (undecorated arch, no tympanum, a little decoration on the imposts of the arch). Otherwise modest Perp. Of interest the arcade between nave and N aisle (of three bays with type-A piers and capitals only to the main shafts), because it is of timber. – The large roundheaded window on the S side is dated 1636. – The N aisle has an original wagon-roof. – FONT. Norman, of cup shape, with cable and concentric semicircles as decoration of the shaft; the

bowl completely plain. – PLATE. Elizabethan Cup by *Jons*
of Exeter ; Paten inscribed *C. Stoneman*, 1691.

OAKFORD

ST PETER. 1838, by *R. S. Pope* (GR), with triple lancet
windows. Only the tower old (with diagonal buttresses
and short pinnacles). – PLATE. Chalice of 1579; small
Waiter on three legs, 1734.

STUCKERIDGE. Nice Late Georgian house with verandahs
on two sides.

OLD BURROW CASTLE *see* LYNTON

ORCHARD
2 m. s of Bratton Clovelly

Farmhouse, but incorporating the remains of a manor
house. A date-stone of 1620 was removed by the late
Sabine Baring Gould to his house at Lew Trenchard,
South Devon. Mullioned granite windows also have gone
there. Only the plan and the masonry remain at Orchard.

ORLEIGH COURT
1½ m. NE of Buckland Brewer

Tudor house in a bad state of repair and recently rather
slumified. The porch is still there with a fine doorway
with branch, leaf, and fleuron decoration in the moulding
of jambs and arch. Above the porch a tunnel-vaulted
chamber. The porch leads into the hall whose hammer-
beam roof remains, with cross-ribs to fill the panels
between beams and purlins (cf. Weare Giffard). The six-
light, one-transome window is Late Tudor, if not later.
At the high-table end Elizabethan panelling transferred
from another part of the house. The staircase behind the
hall is *c.* 1720 with a brick Venetian window and also
balusters elegantly twisted. Alterations were indeed made
by Joseph Davie after 1710 (a date 1721 on firebuckets).

PANCRASWEEK

St Pancras. Isolated on a hill. The N side of the church appears Norman, aisleless, with transept, and in the chancel one small blocked window. The S aisle obviously a Perp addition with three- and four-light Perp windows and an arcade of five bays with granite piers of A type, capitals only to the main shafts, and depressed pointed arches. Richly carved wagon-roofs. Squint from the N transept into the chancel. It cuts into an unexplained, blocked, tall, roundheaded arch. The W tower is unbuttressed and has big cusped pinnacles. – PULPIT. Jacobean. – STAINED GLASS. Bits in the E window, said to come from Muchelney in Somerset.

Thorne: see p. 156.

PARKHAM

St James. Norman S door, similar to Woolsery and Shebbear, with one order of colonnettes and decorated arch. The rest Perp. W tower with thin diagonal buttresses and big polygonal pinnacles, nave and S aisle with arcade of six bays (granite piers of A type, concave octagonal capitals, decorated abaci and nearly semicircular arches). N chancel chapel of three bays of the same design, except that the arches are more pointed. – FONT. Plain, Norman. – COMMUNION RAILS. All balusters twisted. – PLATE. Elizabethan Chalice and Paten of Exeter type, rather crude; Elizabethan Chalice and Paten of 1574; good Bleeding Bowl, London-made, of 1681; Tankard Flagon, Exeter, 1730.

PARRACOMBE

St Petrock. A small church, away from the village which, since 1878, has had its own new church. Early medieval W tower with diagonal buttresses only at the foot, no W door and narrow roundheaded bell-openings. It was struck by lightning and restored in 1908. The exceptional charm of the interior of the church is that it has never been restored. It is still much as it was a hundred and fifty years ago, a rare example of the usual furnishing of a modest village church, poor perhaps, but seemly. When the new church was decided upon, the old was in danger of demolition, but saved by protests and contributions. Ruskin headed the list. The body of the church consists of a C13 chancel (*see* the E window) and Perp nave and S aisle (arcade of four bays with piers of A type, but standard leaf capitals, and depressed pointed arches) with straightheaded windows. The division between nave and chancel is by a SCREEN of the same early type as at Molland, i.e. with no grouping of the mullions of the openings into sections (simply a number of narrow identical lights, each with its own cusped ogee arch), and a straight top to the whole screen. Above it a solid TYMPANUM, such as the post-Reformation Anglican church liked, but as only here and there survives (cf. Molland). The tympanum was repainted in 1758 with the Royal Arms, Commandments, Creed, and Lord's Prayer. – PULPIT. Simply panelled and still provided with sounding board and attached reader's and clerk's pews. – Old completely plain PEWS (C16?), added C18 BOX PEWS rising theatrically at the W end. – FONT. Plain, small, circular bowl, perhaps Norman, said to come from another parish.

CHURCH HOUSE. Just below the church.

INSCRIBED STONE. Romano-British, between Parracombe and Lynton. The inscription reads: CAVVO–FILIUS / C–V–L (?).

PETERS MARLAND

ST PETER. 1868, but the W tower old with buttresses only at the foot, and obelisk pinnacles. – PLATE. Excellent standing Cup, silver-gilt, by *AB*, London, 1595 or 1615, very different from usual Devon plate; Paten and Flagon, 1756.

PETHERWIN, NORTH, *see* NORTH PETHERWIN

PETROCKSTOW

ST PETROCK. Of little architectural interest. Mostly rebuilt 1879 by *J. F. Gould* (GR). Old W tower with diagonal buttresses and obelisk pinnacles. Old N aisle arcade of three bays with octagonal piers and double-chamfered arches. – FONT. Norman, a variety of the table-top type, but one side with two rosettes instead of the blank arcades. Nice Jacobean cover. – PULPIT. Also Jacobean. – STAINED GLASS. Two s windows by *Kempe*, 1891 and 1896. – PLATE. Chalice, Paten, and Flagon, 1682. – MONUMENTS. Two brass tablets to commemorate Sir John Rolle of Stevenstone † 1648 and his ten sons, and Lady Rolle † 1591 and her eight daughters.

PETTON

PETTON CHAPEL. 1848, by *Boyce* of Tiverton. – PLATE. Small chalice on baluster stem by *IM*, *c*. 1635–55.

PILTON

ST MARY. Approached through the pretty imitation-Tudor ALMSHOUSES of 1849. The church formerly belonged to a Benedictine Priory (a cell of Malmesbury), and on the N side the roof-line of adjoining monastic buildings can still be seen, the cloister running along the nave (hence the high sills of the N aisle windows), and other taller buildings butting against the N tower. For the tower is not in the w as usual, but in the N in a position close to the E end, characteristic of this part of North Devon (e.g. Barnstaple) and of an early date. On the ground floor it exhibits large blocked pointed arches to N and E and a stair-turret. To the chancel it opens in a narrow pointed arch with a pretty rib vault, to the N aisle in a tall pointed double-chamfered arch. The whole of this part of the church cannot now be examined, because of the organ. The ground floor chamber was vaulted or meant to be vaulted (*see* the shafts in the corners). On the upper floor the tower has an octagonal storey, a proof that it continued originally or was meant to continue in an octagonal spire. The whole tower was much restored in 1696. The N aisle also belongs to the early buildings. It is separated from the nave by unmoulded pointed arches which look as if they were cut out of the solid wall. The s aisle, on the other hand, is clearly Perp, with piers of A type, leaf capitals only to the main piers and arches almost semi-circular. The four-light windows are renewed; their tracery is exactly as at Barnstaple. – ROOFS. Chancel open-timbered, N aisle wagon-roof now boarded but formerly plastered, said to date from 1639. Wagon-roofs also in s aisle and nave. – FONT COVER. Very handsome with con-cave sides, crocketed and finialed, yet evidently Eliza-bethan. – At the back of the font Early Renaissance panels and bits from a screen, obviously re-used. – PULPIT. Stone, Late Perp, on panelled shaft with panelled body, reticent in taste, as against, for example, the Dartmouth type. – ROOD SCREEN. Across the nave and s aisle. The tracery is A–type standard, except that in the central span-drels of each four-light section there is a different tracery pattern, including three mouchettes in a circle. Coving and cresting gone. The spandrels, where the coving should start, are filled with a jumble of Flamboyant bits. – PARCLOSE SCREEN of three bays with beautifully carved foliage in the spandrels and also an initial R for Raleigh. The chancel chapel is the Raleigh Chapel. – COM-MUNION RAIL across nave and chancel chapel: Eliza-bethan with arches, every second resting on a short column. – PLATE. Elizabethan Chalice and Paten by *Mathew* of Barnstaple; huge silver-gilt Chalice (12 in. tall) by *E. Holaday*, 1713; much good pewter. – MONUMENTS. Sir John Chichester † 1569, big standing wall-monument of good quality, without any figures. Base articulated by short bulgy columns; main storey also with big columns with fine strapwork cartouches between. – Sir Robert Chichester † 1627, also standing wall-monument, this one with life-size kneeling figures. The odd feature is that besides a column on the l. and one on the r. there is one in the centre in front of the prie-dieu towards which the figures kneel. It comes farther forward than the side columns and leads to awkward consequences in the entablature above. – Big and sumptuous epitaph to Chris-topher Lethbridge † 1713 and family.

BULL HOUSE, sw of the church. Tudor house with several original windows, old four-centred arch to the doorway and old battlements.

PILTON HOUSE, se of the church. Large, unadorned, seven-bay, two-storeyed house of c. 1700.

BROADGATE HOUSE, NW of the church. Late c18, though with a few Tudor fragments. s front with three bow-windows, partly Victorianized. In the garden a STANDING STONE, 8 ft high.

PILTON COTTAGE, close to Broadgate House. With pretty iron gates, lower half 1805, upper half 1824.

WESTAWAY, ½ m. NW of the church. The porch of this Neo-Tudorized c18 house comes from Umberleigh Manor House. It is dated 1634.

PORTLEDGE HOUSE
1 m. NW of Alwington Church

Tudor house, very modernized. The windows have lost their stone mullions, the roofs their original gables and pitch and the rooms their plasterwork. Yet the porch remains with its doorway, and the whole carcase too, though gutted to create space for a glazed central hall.

POUGHILL

ST MARY. Unbuttressed, unpinnacled w tower. Nave and N aisle; piers of the arcade of B type with standard capitals, three bays plus a fourth from chancel to chancel chapel, the latter panelled and decorated with fleurons (all extremely renewed). Old wagon-roofs. – BOX PEWS in the aisle.

UPCOTT BARTON. Late medieval house, altered late c16 and c. 1620. Handsome stone front, two-storeyed with symmetrical windows. Timber mullions. (At the E end c15 room with disguised wagon-roof. *Hoskins.*)

PUDDINGTON

ST THOMAS À BECKET. 1838, by *W. Bowden*, of the Devon village type, no longer the arbitrary 'Commissioners'' style. The w tower, old, unbuttressed, unpinnacled. – FONT. Octagonal, Perp, with panelling on shaft and quatrefoils on bowl. – Some of the usual Cornwall–Devon BENCH-ENDS. – PLATE. Plain Cup on baluster stem, 1653; plain Paten on stand by *IM*, 1722.

PUTFORD, EAST, *see* EAST PUTFORD

PUTFORD, WEST, *see* WEST PUTFORD

PYWORTHY

ST SWITHUN. Out of the ordinary run of North Devon churches in several ways. First of all the church has a clerestory (cf. North Molton, Tiverton). Secondly the nave is separated from the s aisle by an arcade of octagonal piers and double-chamfered arches. This arcade, and also the clerestory windows and the chancel windows are no doubt C14, the latter early in the century. The s aisle windows are obviously late Perp. The slim w tower again unusual in that it is strengthened at the foot by angle buttresses. The unceiled wagon-roofs inside are original. – FONT. Plain octagonal. – PLATE. Chalice and Paten by *Jons* of Exeter, 1576; Stoneware Jug with silver mountings in the Elizabethan style; fine pewter pieces.

RACKENFORD

ALL SAINTS. w tower with diagonal buttresses and NE stair-turret. Nave and N aisle of four bays, the piers of the arcade of A type with crude standard capitals, the ornament being mainly abstract. The nave has a ceiled wagonroof supported by crude figures of angels. – FONT. Big, octagonal, Perp, with tracery motifs. – MONUMENT. Arthur Chamberlain † 1941, large wood-carved coat of arms; good.

RACKENFORD MANOR. Plain five-bay two-storeyed Georgian house, enlarged in 1928–32 by *Allan Walton*. He added wings and re-designed the interior almost entirely. The style is Neo-Georgian.

RASHLEIGH BARTON
1 m. NW of Eggesford Station

Farmhouse, but with the remains of the Jacobean manor of
the Clotworthy family, especially two plaster ceilings in
the N wing, the upper one vaulted and amongst the richest
in Devon (cf. Barnstaple). The decoration is unusual, not
ribbed panels, but tendrils and apples, pears, grapes, etc.,
and dogs, cats, pigs, cocks, and even a Pegasus ambling
among them. In the upper room pendants, one of openwork like a bird-cage. Staircase with dog-gate. Painting of
a chimneypiece dated 1611.

ROBOROUGH

ST PETER. 1868, though said to contain original E.E. work.
– PLATE. Elizabethan Chalice and Paten of Barnstaple
type.
COOMBE BARTON: see p. 78.

ROBOROUGH CASTLE see LYNTON

ROMANSLEIGH

ST RUMON. 1868, by *Ashworth*, the W tower 1887, but
apparently built with the old materials. Buttresses only at
the foot. – Scanty remains of St Rumon's HOLY WELL N
of the church.

ROSE ASH

ST PETER. 1888, by *St Aubyn* and *Wadling*, except for the
W tower (low, unbuttressed, unpinnacled) and probably
the arcade between nave and N aisle (piers of A type with
capitals only to the main shafts). – SCREENS. The rood
screen Perp with tracery of B type; coving and cresting
new. The N chancel chapel has on its W and S sides
Jacobean screens, the solid lower panels decorated with
half-wheel motifs, the upper parts with plain long
balusters. Arms of Anne of Denmark and Prince Henry.
Date 1618. – COMMUNION RAILS. Graceful, *c.* 1700–10.
CHURCH HOUSE, S of the churchyard.

ST GILES IN THE WOOD

ST GILES. The W tower Perp (diagonal buttresses at the foot only, low pinnacles), the rest of the church deplorable rebuilding of 1863. – MONUMENTS. Semi-reclining gentleman, bearded, c. 1630; fragment of a larger monument. – Brasses to Alenora Pollard † 1430 (only lower half of the figure preserved); Margaret Rolle of Stevenstone † 1592, larger figure in Elizabethan costume; Joanna Risdon † 1610 with small kneeling figure to the side of an inscription. Other brasses only heraldry and inscriptions.

EBBERLY HOUSE: *see* p. 84.
WAY BARTON: *see* p. 160.
WOODLEIGH BARTON: *see* p. 170.
WINSCOTT: *see* p. 169.

ST GILES-ON-THE-HEATH

ST GILES. Low unbuttressed W tower with modern pyramid roof. Chancel with a small C13 window. – Arcade between nave and S aisle low of five bays, with granite piers of A type, capitals only to the main shafts, decorated abaci and low pointed arches. – FONT. Circular, Norman, undecorated. – BENCH-ENDS. Rather broader in shape than usual, with elementary decoration, two blank cusped arches and above a roundel. The roundels are decorated with rose, fleur-de-lis and also a frontal head. – Former REREDOS. Slate, with Commandments, Creed, and Lord's Prayer, surrounded by minimum decoration of typical c. 1800 character.

SAMPFORD COURTENAY

ST ANDREW. A proud church with W tower and S side all of granite ashlar and all embattled. The tower has the usual Late Perp buttresses of type B and big pinnacles, a broad hood-moulded W door, and a four-light W window. The S side with S porch, a stair-turret at the W end of the aisle, and a lower chancel. The aisle windows of three lights, with pointed arches and Perp tracery, the chancel windows straightheaded without tracery. At the E end of the chancel a one-storeyed extension, also embattled. The chancel E window of five lights has the most elementary panel tracery. The N aisle not granite, not embattled and with straightheaded windows without tracery. Inside, a quite exceptionally wide nave and wide, open aisles. The N arcade of 4 + 1 bays with A-type granite piers, and slightly decorated capitals, the S arcade of 4 + 2 bays has only the last two bays identical with the N; the others are not of granite and have piers of B type with capitals adorned with fleurons. Good wagon-roofs throughout. Amongst the bosses in the chancel a wheel of three rabbits, and a litter of sows may be noted (cf. stone bosses at Exeter Cathedral). – FONT. A variety of the table-top type. – PULPIT. Plain C18. – COMMUNION RAILS. C18, with twisted balusters throughout. – STAINED GLASS. Angels with shields in the tracery of the N aisle E window. – PLATE. Elizabethan Chalice of Exeter type; Paten on stand by *Strang* of Exeter, 1721; Paten by *Stevens* of Launceston, 1731; Flagon by *C. Wright* of London, 1771. It was at Sampford Courtenay that the Devon Rebellion against the vernacular Prayer Book broke out in 1549.

SANDFORD

ST SWITHIN. Perp, except for the low, unbuttressed, unpinnacled W tower. Nave and two aisles of five bays. Piers of B type with standard capitals. Diagonally in one of the piers a niche for an image. Lower chancel. Ceiled wagon-roofs everywhere. – W GALLERY. Returned a little down both aisles. The date is 1657, yet the form still purely Jacobean. – COMMUNION RAIL of c. 1700, re-used as screen to the SW chapel. – REREDOS. Gothic Revival, no doubt of the time of the restoration of the church, i.e. 1847–8. Of the same time the STAINED GLASS in the E window by *Merrick* of Bristol (TK). – BENCH-ENDS. Of the usual Cornwall–Devon type with Early Renaissance ornament, heads in profile, etc., yet said to be Late Elizabethan. – PLATE. Elizabethan Chalice by *Jons* of Exeter; two Tankard Flagons of 1694. – MONUMENTS.

Mary Dowrich † 1604, small brass plate with inscription, recumbent figure on a tomb-chest and l. and r. kneeling figures. – Sir John Davie † 1792, epitaph without figures, quite grand. – Sir Humphrey P. Davie † 1846, with relief of Good Samaritan, by *E. B. Stephens* of Exeter and London.

SCHOOL. Surprisingly grand, with big pediment on heavy attached Tuscan columns; the windows of the front also pedimented. Dated in large figures MDCCCXXV.

DOWRICH HOUSE: *see* p. 81.

(RUKFORD BARTON. Attractive early C17 farmhouse. *Hoskins.*)

SATTERLEIGH

ST PETER. Tiny church, aisleless, with low weatherboarded bellcote. The nave without any N windows. s door original in original wooden frame. The nave is separated from the chancel by a 'tympanum', i.e. a cross-wall originally standing on the (demolished) screen (cf. Molland and Parracombe). The inscriptions on the tympanum Late Georgian. CEILURE above this part of the roof. No visible wagon-roofs otherwise. – FONT. Octagonal, Perp, with quatrefoil panels. – PULPIT. 'Jacobean', but probably mid C17. – BENCH-ENDS. A few, with simple tracery.

SAUNTON

SAUNTON COURT. 1932, by *Lutyens*, as an extension and virtual rebuilding of a farmhouse. Much of the detail looks like a revival of *Lutyens's* early style.

SAUNTON SANDS HOTEL, *c.* 1937, by *Alwyn Underdown*. Modernistic, not genuinely modern, but even that a rarity amongst larger English hotels.

SHEBBEAR

ST MICHAEL. Norman s doorway more ambitious than in the neighbouring villages, one order of colonnettes, but three orders of arch voussoirs, including beak-heads and zigzag. The s aisle arcade has odd square piers with chamfered angles and double-chamfered arches. They could be early C14, the likely date for the tracery of N and s windows. But the windows are all renewed. Do they represent original evidence? w tower with angle buttresses only at the foot, no w door and low pinnacles. s chancel chapel of two bays with the usual A piers of granite with capitals only to the main shafts. Original wagon-roofs in nave, chancel and chancel chapel. – PULPIT. Elizabethan, elaborate with crude figures in the usual arched panels. – PLATE. Sweetmeat Dish, 1659; Almsdish, 1671; Goblet and Flagon, 1788. – MONUMENTS. Unknown Lady, said to be Lady Prendergast of Ludford, not good sculpturally, and not well preserved. – William Rigsby † 1699, nice slate plate with coat of arms, skulls, and hour-glass.

SHEEPWASH

St Lawrence. The church lies behind the village square, with thatched cottages mostly built to the same design. The church 1881 by *J. F. Gould*, tower 1889 by *Webb* of Barnstaple (GR). – FONT. Square, of block-capital shape, one of the semicircular surfaces with foliage, the others plain.

SHEPCOTT BARTON *see* KNOWSTONE

SHIRWELL

St Peter. Short, unbuttressed C13 SE tower with one lancet window and two low pointed unmoulded arches into the inside of the church. The chancel arch is also low and unmoulded and belongs probably also to the C13. On the N side of the church a transept, on the s a later, Perp aisle. The low arcade of three bays has piers of B type with standard leaf capitals. By the N transept an odd rough timber pier as if for a hagioscope from the nave. Open wagon-roofs in chancel, aisle, and N transept, the latter particularly fine. – FONT. Norman, square, of the table-top type, with four flat blank arches to each side of the top. – STAINED GLASS. E window by *Kempe*, 1898. – MONUMENTS. C15 effigy of a lady on a tomb-chest with quatrefoil decoration, in a recess in the chancel N wall, much too low for the figure. – Above it Lady Anne

Chichester † 1723, with two standing figures holding an oval inscription plate under a baldacchino; quality poor. – Frances Lugg † 1712, epitaph with bust at the top; also poor.

SHOULSBURY CAMP see COUNTISBURY

SOUTH MOLTON

The long High Street is divided by an island site beyond which it widens into the Market Place. On the s side the GUILDHALL of 1743, a stone-fronted building of three bays crowned by a cupola. The ground floor with open rusticated arcades, the upper floor with pilasters. Next to the Guildhall the MARKET HOUSE of 1863 in a kind of Italian Renaissance. The island site faces the Market Place with the MEDICAL HALL, which displays an iron verandah on unfluted Ionic columns.

Most houses whitewashed or colour-washed. Some nice Georgian houses in EAST STREET. In East Street also the former HUGH SQUIER'S SCHOOL, a small rectangle of 1684 with two symmetrical arched doors and three (later) Gothic windows.

St MARY MAGDALENE. Reached from the Market Place by a big cast-iron gate between houses. The exterior of the church is distinguished by a tall w tower of four stages, 107 ft high and until 1765 crowned by a spire. The tower has type-B buttresses and tall pinnacles on the battlements. On the s side of the tower a niche with three heads above (sign of the Trinity?). The w door has fleuron decoration, the w window is of four lights. Nave, aisles, transepts and chancel are embattled. The s transept is singled out by quatrefoil decoration of the battlements. The aisle windows are of four lights, mostly with a transome. The interior is unusually light (as Devon churches go) because of the addition of a clerestory to the nave in 1864. The arcades are of five bays with type-B piers, standard Devon capitals, and depressed arches. The capitals have figure as well as leaf carvings. The aisles and shallow transepts are comfortably wide and well lit. The chancel in its masonry is older than the rest of the church and narrower than corresponded to the later proportions. Thus the chancel arch is not wide enough and rests on big corbels to make up for the difference. One of them is a human figure. The chancel chapels open into the chancel with wide, low arches. They are so deep, owing to the thickness of the older chancel walls through which they had to be broken, when the chancel chapels were built that they could be panelled and provided with corbels for statues against the E jambs. The unceiled wagon-roof of the chancel is original. – FONT. Perp, octagonal, shaft panelled, bowl with elaborately cusped quatrefoils. – PULPIT. Stone, octagonal, with narrow leaf-framed panels and figures standing in them under triangularly projecting canopies. – PLATE. Elizabethan Chalice by *Jons* of Exeter; good Tankard Flagon of 1692; Salver of 1727; Almsbowl of 1749. – MONUMENTS. Many, but all minor. HONITON BARTON, 2 m. SE. House of 1676. E-shaped with central porch. Chapel of 1730 behind. *Hoskins*.)

STEVENSTONE HOUSE
2 m. E of Great Torrington

1872–3 by the younger *Charles Barry*. Large, rather grim, derelict at the time of writing. 'The style of architecture may be called Franco-Italian' (*Building News*). Close by fragments of a previous house, probably *c.* 1720–30. Two-storeyed small building of brick with giant Ionic pilasters and hipped roof. Two tiers of arched windows; quoins.

STOCK CASTLE *see* LYNTON

STOCKLEIGH ENGLISH

ST MARY. Perp. Unbuttressed W tower with small pinnacles. Aisleless interior with lower, narrower chancel.

STOKE RIVERS

ST BARTHOLOMEW. Tall W tower with diagonal buttresses, polygonal SE stair-turret and no pinnacles (modern top). Straightheaded N and S windows. Arcade between nave and s aisle of four bays, piers of B type with crude block-like capitals. – FONT COVER. Concave with finial, C17? – PULPIT with Early Renaissance panels. – PANELLING of the C18 along nave and aisle walls. At the same time no doubt the roofs were plastered over inside and provided with cornices. – TILES. A number of Late Gothic tiles by the font. – PLATE. Elizabethan Chalice by *Coton* of Barnstaple; unusually good pewter Flagon. – Much good Late Perp and Early Renaissance woodwork is said to have been ripped out in the C19 and transferred to Weare Giffard house and church *see* p. 160.

STONE BARTON *see* CHAWLEIGH

STOODLEIGH

ST MARGARET. W tower with diagonal buttresses at the foot, no pinnacles, polygonal NE stair-turret. Interior with four-bay arcade between nave and s aisle. Piers of A type with standard Devon leaf capitals. The aisle wagon-roof is original. Chancel and chancel aisle 1880. – FONT. Circular, Norman, with undecorated bowl, but two quaint faces sticking out of the shaft. – PLATE. Elizabethan Chalice and Paten by *Jons* of Exeter; Paten on trumpet stand, probably 1686.

STOODLEIGH COURT. 1882, by *Sir Ernest George & Peto*, in the Tudor style, mixed Early and Later.

STOODLEIGH *see* WEST BUCKLAND

STOWFORD

ST JOHN BAPTIST. Unbuttressed W tower handsomely built with alternating bands of red sandstone and granite. Battlements and big pinnacles. Nave and s aisle, separated by a granite arcade of 3 + 2 bays, the piers of A type with capitals only to the main shafts, decorated abaci and depressed pointed double-chamfered arches. There are a special chancel arch and special arches dividing the s chancel chapel from chancel and aisle. Plain Perp windows. Five original wagon-roofs. The N aisle was added

by *Sir G. G. Scott* in 1874. The chancel chapel was the
family chapel of Haine (*see* p. 92) and a tabard and
gauntlet are exhibited in it. – FONT. Octagonal and odd,
as if it were the late medieval recarving of a Norman font.
– PLATE. Elizabethan Chalice of Exeter type; Cup and
Cover of 1761. – MONUMENTS. Two to members of the
Harris family of Haine, of an ambitiousness unusual in
this district. Christopher Harris and wife erected out of a
will of 1726. Two life-size standing figures with a sarcophagus and obelisk between. The figures are of decidedly
provincial workmanship with painfully short legs, but the
man is all the same in full Roman attire. – John Harris,
† 1770. Sarcophagus in front of an obelisk and on the
pedestal below two portrait medallions.

In the churchyard INSCRIBED STONE to one 'Gunglei. . . .'

SHEPHERDS. House just below the church Porch, general
layout and the slightest indications inside testify to a
Tudor past. Thatched roof and two picturesquely
irregular gables.

STOWFORD HOUSE. Originally the Rectory, with ambitious Neo-Gothic parts of *c.* 1860–70.

HAINE: *see* p. 92.

STUCKERIDGE *see* OAKFORD

SUTCOMBE

ST ANDREW. The oldest part of the church is the W tower,
narrower than the nave, with an unmoulded pointed arch
to the nave and with no W door and no buttresses. The
rest Perp; nave and two aisles, the N and S windows very
late, without tracery. The N arcade of five bays has the
usual granite piers of A type with strip capitals and
depressed pointed arches, the S arcade of only three bays
has the same type of pier, but not of granite, and concave
octagonal capitals to the main shafts only. – FONT.
Octagonal, granite, Perp, with elementary designs. –
PULPIT. With long narrow Early Renaissance panels as
at Welcombe. – SCREEN. Only the wainscoting survives
partly, of an unusual design, with long narrow panels

showing a scroll of broad leaves or a number of square leaves. – BENCH-ENDS. Plenty, with initials, coats of arms, mildly Flamboyant tracery, and Early Renaissance motifs. – TILES. Of the familiar Barnstaple ware, in nave, chancel and s aisle, some larger than usual. – STAINED GLASS. Signs of the Evangelists in the tracery of the chancel E window. – PLATE. Elizabethan Chalice by *Mathew* of Barnstaple; Paten of 1702; two Tankards of 1710. – MONUMENTS. Jonathan Prideaux and Clement Davie, both of the 1760s, and both of the same pretty design.

SWIMBRIDGE

ST JAMES. A small church, but one of considerable interest, especially in its furnishings. The oldest part of the building is the w tower, short and slim, narrower than the nave in front of which it stands. It is unbuttressed and was (probably somewhat later) provided with a broach spire. The spire is lead-covered just like those of Barnstaple and Braunton. As for the church itself, most of it was rebuilt in the C15 and C16. Nave, N and s aisles, chancel, N and s chancel chapels. The arcades differ in design. The N arcade of three bays has piers of the usual Devon B type and standard leaf capitals, the s arcade the same piers but capitals only to the main shafts. The chancel arcades, past the chancel arch, also differ; that in the N is like the N nave arcade, only deeper in the arch-width (cut into the thickness of a pre-existing chancel wall) and more ornate (with 16b figures, for example) in the capitals, that in the s has responds of A type with small capitals. The arch between N aisle and N chancel chapel has one big expressive head-corbel. The chapel was connected with the chancel by a wide hagioscope, where now the vestry has been built in. Externally the s aisle and s porch are embattled; the s and E windows have Perp tracery (s aisle straightheaded), the N windows are of three lights, straightheaded and with mullions to the tops (no arches at all). In his will of 1442 John d'Abernon stated that he wished to be buried in the newly built aisle. This is supposed to refer to the N aisle, but in that case the windows must be a much later alteration.

ROOFS. The wagon-roofs of Swimbridge are specially varied. The oldest is in the chancel, unceiled and un-decorated. The nave roof has bosses (before the restoration of 1880 it was ceiled) and over the rood screen a four-bay-wide CEILURE with cross-ribs. In the S aisle and S chancel aisle there are also bosses and there is even a CEILURE, but only above the E bay. The N aisle has bosses too, and the N chancel chapel a flat ceiling with bosses and cross-ribs.

FURNISHINGS. Uncommonly lavish, perhaps because the church belonged to the Deans of Exeter Cathedral. – FONT. A most extraordinary contraption: lead bowl in octagonal panelled early C18 casing, and folding cup-board doors with Early Renaissance panels between the case and the cover. The cover is an odd mixture of Re-naissance and Gothic elements (much renewed). Above it a canopy with Perp leaf motifs and cross-ribbed and starred ceiling. Is the whole really in its original state? – PULPIT. Stone, cup type as, for example, Dartmouth, with figures of saints (of indifferent sculptural value) under nodding ogee canopies in narrow leaf-framed panels. – SCREEN. One of the most glorious Devon screens: 44 ft long, right across nave and aisles, with tracery of B type, the mullions unusually richly carved, wainscoting of un-usual design with leaf decoration in all its parts, a com-pletely preserved coving with ribs on angel corbels and panels between the ribs which have on the W side finely designed leaf and scroll motifs, not yet in the Italian taste, and on the E side coarser, broader Perp motifs. The cornice a close tangle of nobbly, bossy leaf forms. Where the screen crosses the arcade an opening is left, probaby for a side altar with its reredos, and above this there is a plain forward-curved coving, also with leaf panels. The one on the N side is original, the other restoration. – BENCH-ENDS. A few with large, rather summary tracery (leaf panels). – PLATE. Chalice and Paten of 1576 by *Mathew* of Barnstaple; another smaller Chalice by the

same; Paten of 1718. – MONUMENTS. Tristram
Chichester † 1654, frontal demi-figure, cheek in hand,
in oval niche; deplorably bad. – Epitaph to John Rosier
† 1658, a member of Lincoln's Inn. Therefore the inscription reads:

> Loe with a Warrant sealed by God's decree
> Death his grim Seargant hath arrested me!
> No bayle was to be given: no law could save
> My body from the Prison of the Grave,
> Yet by the Gospell my poore soul hath got
> A Supersedeas, and Death seezed it not, etc.

Charles Cutliffe † 1670, epitaph with a well-painted portrait at the top.

TACKBERE MANOR
1 m. w of Bridgerule Station

Scanty external features from the manor house of the
Gilbert family. Inside, two Jacobean plaster overmantels
and some woodwork also still essentially Jacobean in
character, yet dated as late as 1693.

TADDIPORT
½ m. s of Great Torrington

HOSPITAL CHAPEL of a Leper Hospital mentioned in
1344. Narrow unbuttressed w tower. Nave only 30 ft
long. Above a blocked doorway a three-light Perp window
of oak. No other noteworthy features. The hospital itself
has completely disappeared.

TAPELY PARK
½ m. s of Westleigh

A plain Georgian mansion, heavily Gothicized by *Ewan
Christian* about 1885 and reconstructed in brick with
stone dressings in a grand Edwardian-Neo-Georgian by
Sir John Belcher in 1901. The centre of the s front has a
one-storeyed porch with coupled columns and giant
pilasters with a pediment above. Interiors mostly also by

Belcher, but one late C17 ceiling, and several early C19 ceilings.

TAWSTOCK

St Peter. The church lies on its own in the grounds of Tawstock Court right below the lawn which extends in front of the house. It is one of the architecturally most interesting churches of N Devon. The fact alone that it possesses a tall tower over the crossing singles it out. There are parallels in SE Devon (Crediton, Colyton, Axminster, etc.), but even there only a few. Moreover, most of the visible evidence is of the early C14; the Perp style did little to improve and enlarge the church, and that again is exceptional. Thirdly the activity of the C14 is in some ways so curious and unaccountable that one feels inclined to attribute to the Norman period the core at least of the present plan. The point is this. The early C14 arcades to N and S aisles and the arches between nave and chancel and nave and N and S transepts are all built in such a way that solid unmoulded chunks of masonry are left standing and the mouldings are only applied superficially. The aisle arcade, for example, has square piers only slightly chamfered, with C14 mouldings at the angles, and the arches consist of an unmoulded main part with moulded sub-arches much thinner in section. These rest on separate corbels, some decorated with leaves of *c.* 1300–10 but the majority with heads. It looks, therefore, as if the Dec style pierced earlier walls to add aisles. The same is true of the N, W, and S arches of the crossing. As for windows, the N transept N, and S transept S windows have ogee reticulation typical of *c.* 1320, and the chancel E window has an octofoil above three cusped lights, again early C14. The chancel N windows are in the same style. The view up inside the crossing tower is most remarkable. The square is by squinches of rather plain arches across the corners converted into an octagon, and then again higher up by arches across the angles into a square smaller than the crossing. This area is then covered by a timber rib-vault with a star pattern. The top stage of the tower has two-light Perp bell-openings and thin pinnacles on the battlements. The Perp style also added the two-storeyed vestry, altered the aisle and w windows and extended the s aisle by a chancel aisle of two bays, with piers of B type, standard leaf capitals and depressed pointed arches. There are good open (unceiled) wagon-roofs in nave, chancel, and chancel aisle. The s porch also has a wagon-roof, boarded and with cross-ribs, and in addition, in the place of the s doorway tympanum, a pattern of timber cross-ribs with stars of leaves at the intersections. Where does it come from? The aisle ceilings are of flat pitch with cross-ribs and bosses. They lie higher up than the ceilings or roofs of the early C14 which must have rested on the lower corbel-heads still visible. The wagon-roofs of the transepts were plastered over in the C18 and decorated each with a pretty and very large star of long foliage trails. – ALTAR. In s transept, with an elementary kind of linenfold panelling in the front. Perhaps not originally an altar. The date must be c. 1500 (cf. the hall screen at Bowden, near Berrynarbor). – ROOD SCREEN of unusual design (cf. North Molton). Instead of sections of four lights, there are here on each side of the doorway six individual tall narrow lights, each with its own arched and traceried top. The screen has a square framing and no coving. – PARCLOSE SCREEN with standard tracery, but the doorway with spandrels decorated with coarsely carved Renaissance profiles in roundels. – PEW in s transept, a very remarkable object, small with two solid back-walls panelled, and a complete ceiling with rosettes. The decoration, especially the thick balusters, is decidedly in the Franco-Flemish Early Renaissance taste, no doubt earlier than 1550. – TOWER GALLERY high up in the s transept to connect the stair-turret with the central tower: the parapet with good Perp decoration, but probably not originally in that position. – BENCH-ENDS. Not many, all with Early Renaissance motifs, one with the arms of Henry VIII, another with a one-armed, one-legged monster (one of the 'hinky-punks' of Dartmoor?). – TILES. Of Barnstaple type, in the s chancel chapel – SUN DIAL.

Outside the s porch, by *John Berry*, 1757, showing the
time in the principal capitals of Europe, and also, for
example, at Cairo, Babilon, and Port Royal. – ALTAR
CLOTH. Embroidered, s transept, 1697. – HOUR GLASS
STAND in the form of an arm in parvise above vestry. –
MONUMENTS (in chronological order). Wooden C14
effigy of a lady in a recess in the N chancel wall, perhaps
Eleanor or Margaret Martin. The Martins held the
manor of Tawstock until in the mid C15 it passed into the
hands of the mighty Bourchier family. John Bourchier,
Lord Fitzwarren, was created Earl of Bath in 1536. –
Frances Lady Fitzwarren, 1589, s chancel chapel, six- 34
poster with recumbent effigy and good strapwork decoration. – Sir John Wray † 1597, N transept, slate-covered
tomb-chest with large slate back-plate showing kneeling
figures, cartouche and achievement. The monument was
transferred to Tawstock from St Ive, nr Callington in
Cornwall, in 1924, a Wray having married a Bourchier in
1652. The Wrays were the successors of the Bourchiers at
Tawstock. – Thomas Hinson † 1614 and wife, s chancel
chapel, epitaph with the usual kneeling figures facing each
other. Hinson was Surveyor and Receiver General to the
third Earl and married a 'Cosyne Germain'. – William
Bourchier, 3rd Earl of Bath † 1623, chancel, a sumptuous 36a
standing wall-monument of alabaster, with recumbent
effigies on a sarcophagus, frontally kneeling smaller
figures to heads and feet, a big strapwork cartouche with
inscription behind, and a far projecting cornice with semi-
circularly rising centre (a first-class work of its date). –
Mary St John † 1631, chancel, epitaph with kneeling
figure. – William Skippon † 1633, chancel, epitaph with
kneeling figure. Skippon was steward and treasurer to the
3rd Earl. – Henry Bourchier, 5th Earl of Bath, † c. 1680,
s chancel chapel, a splendid relatively restrained, free-
standing monument of white and black marble. Big base
on which four seated dogs support a big square bulging
sarcophagus. At the four corners four black obelisks. –
Lady Rachel Fane, wife of the 5th Earl, † 1680, s chancel 37a
chapel, life-size standing figure of white marble, in heavy

robes. Mrs Esdaile has discovered that the monument is
an exact copy of the statue of the Countess of Shrewsbury
at St John's College, Cambridge. This was made in 1672
by *Thomas Burman* († 1674). Mrs Esdaile attributes the
Tawstock figure to his son, *Balthasar Burman*. – Sir
Henry Northcote † 1729, N transept, by *Thomas Jewill* of
Barnstaple; nothing special. – Mary Lady Wray † 1751,
S transept, with white and pink marble sarcophagus on
rocaille feet, very handsome. – Ann Chilcot † 1758, wife
of Thomas Chilcot, organist of Bath, N transept, also a
fine piece of its date, with the inscription surmounted by
a tondo with a seated allegorical figure, and above that the
usual obelisk with the profile portraits of husband and
wife in one roundel. The inscription plate commemorating him was never filled in. – Sir Bourchier Wray † 1784,
S transept, stately, absolutely plain free-standing urn on a
big square pedestal. – Ann Lady Wray † 1791, by *King* of
Bath, with a standing woman by an urn below two sprigs
of weeping willow. – Ann Bourchier Wray † 1813, also
with a female by an urn. – Many still lesser epitaphs by
Gould and *Youing* of Barnstaple, *Stephens* of Exeter, etc.

45 TAWSTOCK COURT. Thatched lodges at the entrances with
tree-trunk verandahs. Of the Tudor mansion only the
39b gatehouse remains, with two polygonal turrets and the
gateway itself with a four-centred arch. Date-plate 1574.
The house has a Victorianized W front which seems still
to retain the plan of the Tudor house, a principal S front
facing the church which was rebuilt after a fire in 1787, in
the Gothick of the moment, i.e. symmetrical, castellated,
with angle turrets, and in the centre a castellated pediment. The N side all redone in 1885.

TAWTON, NORTH, *see* NORTH TAWTON

TETCOTT

Church and house lie close together, without the proximity
of a village.

HOLY CROSS. Unbuttressed W tower with cusped pinnacles. Red stone with an occasional band of granite. On

the N side of the church several narrow C13 windows. In the S transept also narrow cusped lancet. – FONT. Norman, circular with a top border of crosses saltire. The base more elaborate than the bowl (cf. Clawton); corner faces and half rosettes between, as if it had originally been a font of the Cornish St-Thomas-by-Launceston type. – PEW RAILS of the Arscott Chapel, fine openwork carving of *c.* 1700. – BENCH-ENDS. Broader than usual, with elementary decoration.

TETCOTT HOUSE. Interesting house of 1603 (date on the S porch) and *c.* 1700. Of the latter building much has been pulled down, but the sash windows remain, a fine brick chimneystack, and some brick outbuildings (dovecote, laundry). The earlier building had an enclosed courtyard. There are also several mullioned granite windows, the heavily beamed ceiling of the hall, and a plaster fireplace (now partly destroyed) in the room above the hall. The view from the W with the various roofs and gables is exceedingly picturesque.

THELBRIDGE

ST DAVID. 1872. – PLATE. Late Elizabethan Chalice and Paten; Flagon, 1737; plain plate Paten, 1791.

THORNBURY

ST PETER. A good deal of the early medieval church remains. Unbuttressed low W tower a little narrower than the nave. Nave, S transept, chancel. Late Norman S doorway with two orders of colonnettes, the capitals partly scalloped, partly with volutes. The arch with two roll mouldings. A Perp N chancel chapel added to the chancel somewhat later (octagonal piers, double-chamfered arches), and a N aisle yet later, in the C15: two bays with the usual granite piers of A type. – Bits from SCREEN and BENCH-ENDS re-used in the chancel seats. – Spicott MONUMENT, probably to Sir John Spicott † 1641; sadly mutilated; only the recumbent figures, in bad preservation, four kneeling smaller figures and two relief medallions survive.

THORNE

1 m. E of Pancrasweek Church

Farmhouse with uncommonly interesting C14 remains of a manorial chapel, licensed in 1377, 1381, and 1400: a doorway, a tall two-light window and the hood-mould of another window of the same size.

THRUSHELTON

St George. In a pretty, sheltered position just above a stream. Unbuttressed w tower with rectangular NE stairturret; the windows of the church all straightheaded except the two in the E. S aisle separated from the nave by a two-bay arcade with octagonal piers, the plainest capitals and double-chamfered arches. The chancel arch of the same moulding. Only the S chancel chapel has the more usual arches of A type (with decorated abaci) towards nave and aisle. Original wagon-roof in the aisle.

TORRINGTON, BLACK, *see* BLACK TORRINGTON
TORRINGTON, GREAT, *see* GREAT TORRINGTON
TORRINGTON, LITTLE, *see* LITTLE TORRINGTON
TORR STEPS *see* EXMOOR

TRENTISHOE

St Peter. A minute church, especially before the present chancel was built in 1861. It stands in no village, just by a farmstead in a sheltered fold below the bare downs, with the sea less than half a mile to the NW. Tiny, narrow w tower, narrower than the nave and now almost merging into the hillside. No aisles. Inside, a musicians' gallery of 1771 is preserved, with a hole in the parapet where the double-bass needed space beyond the narrow confines of the gallery. The tympanum between nave and chancel (cf. Molland, Parracombe) has disappeared. – PLATE. Elizabethan Chalice and Paten, not of a usual Devon type.

TWITCHEN

In a lonely position, high up, and facing Exmoor.

St Peter. 1844, by *Hayward*, except for the low unbuttressed w tower. Inside, FONT. Norman, circular, with plain elementary decoration.

UMBERLEIGH
1 m. N of Atherington

Umberleigh Manor no longer exists (cf. Atherington), but, according to Mr G. W. Copeland, a good C13 doorway and the remains of two lancet windows remain of the CHAPEL.

UPCOTT

The Mansion is dated 1752 on a rainwater-head. It belonged to the Harris family (cf. Pilton). The s front of nine bays, two-storeyed, with a central three-bay pediment in which rather awkwardly a Venetian window appears. One-storeyed deep Tuscan four-column porch. Except for the staircase with timber balusters little of the original interiors remains. – Much lower down towards the estuary of the Taw a castellated sham gatehouse, built no doubt as an 'eye-catcher'.

UPCOTT BARTON *see* POUGHILL

UPLOWMAN

St Peter. From a C14 church one moulded capital preserved in the s porch. The next church was built *c.* 1500 by the Lady Margaret (Margaret Beaufort, mother of Henry VII: *see* Sampford Peverel). This church was almost completely rebuilt in 1864 (chancel added). The arcade between nave and s aisle with piers of B type and standard capitals and especially the arch for a tomb-chest between chancel and s chancel chapel look original. The w tower, unbuttressed, embattled but unpinnacled, is definitely part of the medieval, probably the C14, church.

Widhayes Farm. C17 gatehouse with original studded door.

UPTON HELIONS

St Mary. Surrounded by only a few houses. Unbuttressed, unpinnacled w tower with NE stair-turret. s porch attached to w end of s aisle. Lower chancel. The windows mostly three-light, straightheaded. s door Norman, simple, with one inserted order, the capitals scalloped. Unmoulded tower arch, unmoulded chancel arch. The three-bay arcade between nave and aisle with piers of unusual section: lozenge-shaped with four shafts in the main directions; very plain capitals. Ceiled wagon-roofs. – FONT. Norman, in the shape of a big block-capital. – BENCH-ENDS. Of the usual Cornwall–Devon type with foliage motifs. On one of them a lion *couchant*. – PLATE. Very fine Beaker with Cover, *c.* 1600, standing on three lions, the bowl decorated in *repoussé* with scenes from the Life of the Virgin. – MONUMENT. Richard Reynell † 1631 and wife, epitaph with the traditional kneeling figures (quite big) facing each other.

WADLAND BARTON
1 m. s of Ashbury

E-shaped manor house, supposed to have a date 1568 inside. One low four-light timber-framed window survives.

WARKLEIGH

St John the Evangelist. Not in a village, close only to a farm. Tallish w tower with diagonal buttresses and pinnacles. s aisle opened in three bays to the nave. The piers of B type with capitals only to the main shafts. The fourth bay opens into the s chancel chapel, a family chapel, with larger windows than the rest of the church. The arch to the chancel broader than the others so that a large squint
29 can go through its w pier. – BENCH-ENDS with Renaissance foliage and profile heads in medallions, the usual motifs; made into a screen under the w tower arch. –
30a PULPIT. C18. – CIBORIUM. A most interesting object, of a kind, very rare, if not unique in England. A wooden box to carry the Blessed Sacrament for administration to the

sick. The box is 7¾ by 7¼ in. on a moulded base. The sides
are painted with roses, a sun in a circle and typically, Perp
leaves in the spandrels. The colours are green, red, white,
and gold. – PLATE. Elizabethan Chalice and Paten by
Mathew of Barnstaple.

WASHFIELD

ST MARY. Architecturally of little importance. The usual
W tower of the district, with diagonal buttresses, NE
stair-turret and no pinnacles. The arcade of three bays
with A-type piers and capitals only to the four main
shafts, plus one arch from chancel into chancel chapel
with standard leaf capitals. – FONT. Norman, square, of
table-top type, one side of the top with six blank arches,
the others with similarly elementary zigzag decoration.
– SCREEN. 1624, rich Jacobean style workmanship;   23b
the openings divided by Corinthian columns, not by
balusters, the cornice decoration with animal and foliage
motifs, not with strapwork; crowning Royal Arms. –
PLATE. Chalice of 1606; Paten on foot, 1714. – MONU-
MENTS. Brass plate to Henry Worth † 1606, with kneeling figures, the small plate in a stone frame with coupled
columns.

BROOKE. Farmhouse, the S side with small mullioned
straightheaded windows, and an oriel window high up.
This is boldly inscribed and dated 1564.

WASHFORD PYNE

ST PETER. 1882, by *R. M. Fulford*, with a few quite original
features, notably the S transept front and the N nave windows. – PLATE. Chalice by *Jons* of Exeter, 1575.

WATERMOUTH CASTLE
1 m. N of Berrynarbor

Big castellated mansion of 1825, much Victorianized, with a
splendid wide view over the sea to the N. In the sub-
tropical gardens (now very neglected) an ARCH consisting
of elaborately decorated stonework panels from the porch
of Umberleigh House (not from Berrynarbor, as the

printed literature says). One panel has the date 1525; others with Flamboyant wheels, shields, etc. The original porch must have been quite an exceptional showpiece.

WAY BARTON
2 m. NE St Giles in the Wood

The only interesting fragment of the medieval house is a (composite) stone set into the front wall of the farmhouse. It shows the heads of two ladies wearing wimples (i.e. late C13 or early C14) and the smaller head of a man between and above them. Were they corbels?

WEARE GIFFARD

HOLY TRINITY. W tower with diagonal buttresses and no pinnacles. Nave and S aisle. The arcade (five bays), quite uncommon in the neighbourhood, has piers of B type (with concave capitals). The window tracery on the S as on the N side equally unusual. Two-light windows have depressed arches as tops of each light and a semicircular arch to cover both lights, with the pointed arch above. Three-light windows have the same design with the result that the semicircular arches intersect. – FONT. Square, Norman, with scalloped under side. – BENCH-ENDS. A few of the usual type and designs. – S DOOR original. – STAINED GLASS. Many old bits in the window tracery. In the S aisle E window remains of a C15 Jesse window.* – PAINTING. Martyrdom of St Edmund, against S wall, badly preserved, Tudor or later. – MONU-MENTS. Cross-legged knight, lady wearing wimple, both c. 1300, both slim and probably of high quality when their original surface still existed. – Four generations of Fortescues, 1638, epitaph with two frontally kneeling figures, two kneeling figures in profile above, and masses of children in small panels and medallions by the side. – Eleanor Fortescue † 1847, tomb-chest with brass cross and inscription on the lid.

38 WEARE GIFFARD HALL. Four periods appear, late C15,

* Other bits of the same in the manor house.

late C16 and, alas, the early and the late C19. The then owner in 1832 restored the house and filled the rooms with a tantalizing jumble of panelling, posts of four-poster beds, overmantels, etc., just close enough to what the house might originally have contained to deceive even a canny observer. The great historical importance of Weare Giffard lies in the contribution of the C15, i.e. a good deal of the external appearance; the gatehouse and especially the hall with its screen (lower storey), its tall dais window to the S, its huge fireplace close to that window and its splendid hammerbeam roof. The hall is not large, and the luxuriousness of the roof is all the more impressive. The wall-plate has a broad band of magnificent foliage. Seated animals are on the hammerbeams; curved braces, richly cusped and with pendants, crossed wind-braces between principals and purlins. There is nothing in Devon secular architecture to emulate it. It is unfortunate that (some time later in the C19) the windows of the hall and nearly all others were drastically renewed. The linenfold panelling in the hall is topped by Early Renaissance panelling of c. 1540. Other panels of the same date and type occur in other rooms. High up against the W wall Royal Arms of 1599. That date may apply to the Elizabethan panelling and decoration of other rooms, e.g. one in the SE wing. The panelling here very similar to Hartland Abbey. The parapet of the Minstrels' Gallery of the hall has also Late Elizabethan panelling (but only on the E face). On the W face towards the hall there is some C17 church panelling instead, mischievously brought in (it is said from Stoke Rivers Church). The main staircase also an 1832 addition with carving of two different periods. Even more puzzling is the W porch, consisting of two large splendidly carved arches, both rather too large to have originally belonged to the house. But they carry all the appropriate coats of arms, besides being finely carved along jambs and voussoirs, though not as exquisitely as the original front doorway at the S end of the screen. This has a tree trunk instead of the usual tendril, and leaves scrolling round it. The general shape of the house is a central range with the

N.D.—6

hall in its centre, two long projecting wings to the s and a courtyard, originally closed, apparently irregularly, to the N.

WELCOMBE

The setting here is entirely N Cornish, complete with the little HOLY WELL SE of the church, and the dedication to

ST NECTON. Early W tower, i.e. low, without buttresses and W door, and with tiny round-arched bell-openings. Early plan, aisleless, but with N and S transepts. All windows altered. Wagon-roof with parts of richly decorated wall-plate. – PULPIT. With narrow Early Renaissance panels as at Sutcombe. – SCREEN. The most important feature of the church, supposed to be one of the earliest timber screens in Devon: tall single-light panels arranged in sections of four. Each light roundheaded and round-cusped. Straight top, no coving or special cornice. The foliage friezes of the present cornice appear to be later. The wainscoting is unfortunately made up of discarded bench-ends. – LECTERN. Jacobean; quite a rarity. – READER'S DESK. Interesting, with tracery ends and simple poppy-heads. – PLATE. Cup of London make, 1653; Salver on three legs, 1751.

WEMBWORTHY

ST MICHAEL. Virtually C19, but for the tower at the W end of the S aisle which is of 1626 (unbuttressed except at the foot, unpinnacled). The wagon-roof also seems old. – PLATE. Good Elizabethan Chalice of Exeter type; Chalice, Patens, Almsdish, and Flagon by *Grundy*, London, 1769.

HILL FORTS, Iron Age, at the N and S ends of the village.

WERRINGTON

WERRINGTON PARK was the residence of the Abbots of Tavistock. It was then given by Henry VIII to John Lord Russell, and passed from the Russells to Sir Francis Drake who rebuilt the house *c.* 1620. The house, incorporating Tudor remains, is quite large with a central porch facing s and two lower wings also towards s. It has the usual granite windows with several mullions and no outstanding interior features. It is now hidden behind the new mansion built by a Morice early in the C18, after the estate had, in 1651, come into the hands of Sir William Morice. For the C18 mansion, or a part of its garden, the medieval church had to be demolished. The new church was erected half a mile NW (*see* below). The best craftsmen were employed for the new mansion. The name of the architect is unknown, but it may well have been *Kent* himself. The house is of seven bays width with a central bay-window. There is no external decoration at all except the emphasizing of a few windows and the door. The roof-pitch cannot be original. Is it an Early Victorian alteration? The plan is eminently simple and clear: three front rooms, a wide corridor behind, right through the house, ending in a Venetian window, the staircase and other rooms behind the corridor. The same long corridor on the upper floor. The decoration of the main rooms is superb. As the house passed into the hands of the Duke of Northumberland in 1775 and medallions of the Duke and Duchess appear in the plasterwork of the staircase, it is quite possible that decoration was continued through all those years. The stucco work of the staircase (three flights round an open wall) is in a slightly earlier style than that of the state rooms (in which French *rocaille* appears). The fireplaces are in the *Kent* style.

In the grounds on a hill an eye-catcher, a folly with a seat in a deep round-arched recess and with three Indian sugar-loaf excrescences on top. The former may well be derived from the Daniells' Indian drawings and aquatints, which would date this addition to the alterations of Werrington Park *c*. 1800 or shortly after.

ST MARTIN. Built in 1742 (*see* above) and with its original earliest Gothic Revival front quite possibly a design by *William Kent*. The old tower was re-used (diagonal buttresses and pinnacles) but the façade was considerably widened by a screen-wall with angle turrets, all castellated and provided with the typical blank quatrefoils of

C18 Gothicism. In niches in the façade and on the other sides of the church contemporary statues of the crudest style, yet at the same time quite impressive in their wild attitudes. The interior of the church is completely redone. – FONT. Norman, undecorated, but on a base with heads at the corners. – Another FONT with small bowl on baluster shaft is contemporary with the building of the church. – PLATE. Elizabethan Chalice and Paten of Exeter type. – MONUMENT to some members of the Drake family: kneeling figures in relief in a strapwork frame.

BRIDGE. Yealm Bridge s of Werrington (*see* Cornwall).

BRIDGE. River Attery, carrying a private drive to Werrington Park; C18.

BRIDGE. River Tamar, on way to Druxton; four arches, *c.* 1520.

WEST ANSTEY

ST PETROCK. Small, with w tower (diagonal buttresses, no pinnacles, NE polygonal stair-turret), inner arcade between nave and N aisle with A-type piers and standard Devon leaf capitals. – FONT. Norman, of tub shape, with saltire cross and palmette decoration, similar to Bishopsteignton. – BENCH-ENDS. A few of the usual Cornwall–Devon type. – STAINED GLASS. Fragments in the s chancel window (Crucifixus, etc.). – PLATE. Chalice of *c.* 1600; Paten of 1725 on stand of 1721.

WESTAWAY *see* PILTON

WEST BUCKLAND

ST PETER. 1860, by *R. D. Gould* of Barnstaple, with the exception of the Perp w tower with diagonal buttresses and no pinnacles. Close to the s porch a set of slate HEADSTONES with very pretty inscriptions (by *T. Britton*). – PLATE. Elizabethan Chalice by *Mathew* of Barnstaple.

DEVON COUNTY SCHOOL, ½ m. E. 1861, by *R. D. Gould*; later much enlarged (hall and dormitories 1878; workshop 1935).

STOODLEIGH, ¾ m. N. Five-bay, two-storey, plain stone house with hipped roof. The date 1731 on a fireplace.

WESTCOTT BARTON see MOLLAND

WESTDOWN

HOLY TRINITY. Early plan, not enlarged by Perp aisles. N and S transepts, the S transept opening into the nave in an unmoulded pointed arch, the N transept in a more ambitious heavy double-hollow-chamfered arch. The N transept has a good open wagon-roof of trefoil section and in its N wall a three-light early C14 window with ogee reticulation (just like Tawstock); also below it, a low tomb recess, decorated with bell-flower and containing a timber EFFIGY, man with folded hands, details now unrecognizable. It commemorates probably Sir John Stowford, who founded a chantry in the church, was born in 1290 and still alive in 1372. Of the same date as the effigy and the window the fine pointed cinquefoil-cusped PISCINA, transferred, it is said, from the transept to the chancel. The W tower alone looks decidedly Perp with buttresses of type B and small pinnacles. It was rebuilt in 1772. The N chancel chapel and most of the windows are C19. – FONT. Norman, raw, as if the decoration has been hacked off. – PLATE. Chalice probably by *Coton* of Barnstaple, 1575. – MONUMENT. Epitaph to Francis Isaac † 1658 and wife, with two frontal demi-figures holding hands, against one common double-arched recess.

WESTLEIGH

ST PETER. W tower with thick buttresses covering the angles, polygonal stair-turret on the S side close to the E angle, no pinnacles. The chancel windows look *c.* 1300 but are renewed. S porch and S door a little later. N aisle Perp, with granite piers of A type, capitals only to the main shafts, and depressed pointed arches. – TILES. In nave and aisle; not only the usual Barnstaple designs. – PAINTINGS. Christ, *c.* 1830, by *Harlow*. 'Rizpah' by *Lord Leighton*, exhibited at the Royal Academy in 1893,

and the typical Chantrey Bequest picture. – MONU-
MENTS. Several to the Cleoland family of Tapely, especially John † 1763 (profile in medallion above a flat very
classical urn), and Augustus † 1849 (by *M. W. Johnson*
of New Road, London) with a large weeping figure on her
knees below a weeping willow.

TAPELY PARK: *see* p. 150.

WEST MOLLAND *see* MOLLAND

WEST PUTFORD

ST STEPHEN. An early medieval plan, aisleless, with N
transept. Windows in the chancel, the transept and the
nave point to *c.* 1300. The W tower is unbuttressed and
has stunted pinnacles. – FONT. Circular, Norman, rather
shapeless, with one cable-moulding between bowl and
shaft. – PULPIT. C18 with twisted balusters. – COM-
MUNION RAILS. C18 with twisted balusters. – BENCH-
ENDS. Only a few old bits. – TILES. On the chancel; of the
usual Barnstaple designs. – PLATE. Late C16 Wine Cup
with tree and leaf decoration; Paten, a Taster Dish,
signed *I.D.*

CHURSTON MANOR. Elizabethan manor house built by a
member of the Prideaux family some time between 1576
and 1611. Hall with four-light window, original screen,
and overmantel with two allegorical figures in Elizabethan dress, representing Peace and Plenty, sculpturally very crude (cf. Boringdon, South Devon).
Another plaster overmantel in an upper room. The
granite porch is an incongruous addition from Ashbury
House where it was a gateway. It was removed to
Churston in 1934.

WESTWARD HO!

Murray's *Handbook* in 1872 says 'Westward Ho! consists at
present of two or three rows of terraces, many scattered
villas, a single line of shops, and a church nearly opposite
the principal hotel. . . . A single farmhouse alone existed
before the "Company" was founded for the purpose of

creating a new watering-place.' The landmarks of 1870 are all still there, monuments to the nadir of light-heartedness in English architecture, and therefore singularly unsuited to a seaside resort. The yellow brick of N Devon does not help matters either. The church (HOLY TRINITY, 1867) is by *W. L. Oliver* (GR).

WEST WOOLFARDISWORTHY (WOOLSERY)

HOLY TRINITY. W tower with thick buttresses hiding the angles, and unmoulded pointed arch towards the nave, and centrally placed polygonal stair-turret on the S side, unusual in N Devon but not infrequent in the S of the county. Witnesses of the Norman church are the surviving S transept and S door. This has one order of colonnettes and decorated arch orders: the central one with beakheads and the inner one with zigzag (exactly as at Shebbear). Interior with wide nave and a five-bay arcade to the N aisle which has granite piers of A type, capitals only to the main shafts, decorated abaci, and unusually wide depressed pointed arches. An inscription records a rebuilding in 1648. This is probably responsible for the cornices of the completely plastered-over wagon-roofs. – FONT. Square, Norman, undecorated, on five shafts of blue stone. – BENCH-ENDS. Of the usual Devon and Cornwall type, a good many of them. Decorated with shields with arms or with initials, figures of saints, Christ crucified (very unusual) and also some of the Instruments of the Passion (ladder, nails, scourge, etc.). – MONUMENTS. Richard Cole † 1614, standing wall-monument with semi-reclining figure, propped on elbow, columns to l. and r., and obelisks and achievement on top; sculpturally not good. – Several later epitaphs, e.g. Richard Hammett and wife with a plain urn against an obelisk; anonymous, *c.* 1790.

WEST WORLINGTON

ST MARY. Picturesque access to the churchyard under the archway of the former Church House. Picturesque, crooked, shingled spire on the short unbuttressed tower stump. Nave and s aisle separated by a three-bay arcade with B-type piers with standard Devon capitals with figures (angels) as well as the usual leaf decoration. s aisle and s porch with original wagon-roofs. – PARCLOSE SCREEN with standard type A tracery and spandrel decoration. – BENCH-ENDS fairly plain. – PLATE. Paten of 1723; good pewter Flagon. – MONUMENT. Epitaph to Sir Thomas Stucley † 1663 (cf. Chawleigh).

AFFETON BARTON: *see* p. 38.

WHITECHAPEL BARTON
2½ m. ENE of South Molton

E-shaped two-storeyed manor house originally of the Bassett family. Several Elizabethan windows with wooden mullioned frames. Inside, the contemporary screen survives, and the door to the staircase.

WIDHAYS *see* UPLOWMAN

WINKLEIGH

ALL SAINTS. Perp throughout. w tower with buttresses only at the foot. Top with cusped pinnacles. Exterior of the body of the church much renewed. Built into the wall a Norman (?) head. The s transept (Gidley Chapel) added early in the C17. The N side of the N aisle is the show-front towards the village. The windows big, of three lights, and buttresses between them; the N transept embattled. The arcade between nave and N aisle of five bays with granite piers of A type; capitals only to the main shafts; nearly semicircular arches. An additional bay opens into the chancel chapel. The piers here have a different moulding which is repeated in the chancel arch and one side of the arch to the N transept (four main shafts and four subsidiary shafts in the diagonals). Original open wagon-roofs. – STAINED GLASS. Bits in one w window (angels with shields). – PLATE. Almsdish 1684; Chalice and Paten by *Whipham & Wright*, 1763 faintly medievalizing.

WINSCOTT
1½ m. E of St Giles in the Wood

Cheerless Gothic mansion by *William White*, 1864.

WINSFORD *see* HALWILL

WITHERIDGE

St JOHN BAPTIST. Quite large compared with most of the churches in this singularly barren neighbourhood. The W tower Perp, originally with shingled spire. Upper stage rebuilt 1841. The W window a characteristic example of latest Perp tracery. Of 1841 also probably the battlements of the body of the church, the slightly funny embattled priest's door and the generally much renewed-looking appearance of the church. – Nave and two aisles with four-bay quite tall arcades; the piers of B type with standard capitals. Squint from the S aisle. The chancel earlier (E.E. S window; the E window, however, 1877). It is separated from the nave by a chancel arch. Ceiled wagon-roof in the nave. S doorway elaborately decorated with fleurons on jambs and arch; niche for an image above. – FONT. Perp, octagonal, quite richly decorated, mainly with quatrefoils. – PULPIT. Stone, Perp, with figures in narrow panels under nodding ogee canopies. In one panel a badly carved Crucifixion. The style no doubt later than 1500.

WITHLEIGH

St CATHERINE. 1847, by *Hayward*. No tower, no aisles.

WONHAM
1 w. SW of Washford Pyne

Of the Manor House nothing survives; of the CHAPEL just two sharply pointed window-heads with two-light Perp tracery.

WOODBARROW ARMS *see* EXMOOR

WOODLEIGH BARTON
1½ m. s of St Giles in the Wood

Of the medieval Manor House the CHAPEL is recognizable, at the end of a projecting N wing: doorway, E window and two blocked S windows.

WOOLACOMBE

ST SABINUS. 1911, by *Caroë*, small but quite worthy of the architect of St David at Exeter. Red sandstone with asymmetrically placed tower stump covered by a saddleback roof, and big roof covering the nave and the narrow lean-to aisles (N aisle not yet built). The aisles have low three-light windows, the chancel is slightly narrower than the nave, but also has aisles, separated from the chancel by oak posts stained green. Tall chancel screen. Fine open roof with big semicircular braces.

WOOLFARDISWORTHY (EAST)

ST MARY. 1845, by *Hayward*. – PLATE. Elizabethan Chalice by *T. Mathew* of Barnstaple. The Paten seems to be worked into an Almsdish (dated 1600); Paten and Flagon by *Elston* of Exeter, 1728.

WOOLFARDISWORTHY NR BIDEFORD, see WEST WOOLFARDISWORTHY

WOOLSERY see WEST WOOLFARDISWORTHY

WORLINGTON, EAST, see EAST WORLINGTON

WORLINGTON, WEST, see WEST WORLINGTON

WORTHAM
2 m. SSW of Bratton Clovelly

No doubt one of the most remarkable houses of its size in Devon. It can still convey a fairly complete impression of an Early Tudor manor house. The shape is that of an L, the larger arm with a porch and fairly symmetrical fenestration l. and r. of it. The wall of freestone ashlared. The straightheaded windows of several lights also have still pointed or depressed rounded tops to the individual lights. At the back is a polygonal stair-turret. Inside, the hall has a complete C15 screen with pinnacles, a most unusual feature. The hall is low with linenfold panelling, a ceiling with moulded beams, and Perp leaf decoration and the room above it has an open roof with cross-braces between the beams and purlins. Both rooms have their original fireplaces. In the room beyond the screen (where one would expect the offices) is Elizabethan panelling, but a delightful ceiling with cross-ribs and bosses like the 'ceilure' above the rood screen in a church.

YARNSCOMBE

St Andrew. Norman N transept tower (cf. Exeter Cathedral), low, with low (later) pinnacles and a polygonal stair-turret on the w side. Arch to the nave low, pointed and unmoulded. Perp s aisle added to the nave, with four-bay granite arcade, piers of A type, depressed pointed arches. Old ceiled wagon-roofs. – FONT. Big, octagonal, Perp with tracery, quatrefoil, etc., patterns. – CHEST. Early, iron-bound. – TILES. Of the usual Barnstaple designs, in the s aisle, E end. – STAINED GLASS. C14 angel with shield, s aisle, E window. – PLATE. Elizabethan Chalice, style of *T. Mathew*; Paten by the same, 1609 (the earliest paten proper in the county, as against other chalice covers). – MONUMENTS. Two C15 recesses, one in the chancel N wall, the other in the aisle s wall, both with depressed pointed arches, the chancel one much more elaborate, with panelled back-wall and a little seated figure in the centre. The tomb-lid with a long inscription to John Cookworthy † 14— (last figures illegible) and wife. – John Pollard † 1667 and family, with frontal heads in roundels.

YEO VALE
2 m. N of Buckland Brewer

Ruins of a Perp church. The chancel with its Perp windows, the N transept, N door and s aisle are easily recognizable. The most probable explanation of this ruin between the trees is that it was originally the chapel of Yeo Vale House in the valley opposite (where just one porch remains of the big medieval mansion, rebuilt in Georgian times) and was re-erected as an essay in the Picturesque. The chapel of Yeo Vale House was licensed in 1375 and again in 1406.

YOULSTON

½ m. w of Shirwell

The house looks Palladian–Early-Georgian and contains plasterwork of *c.* 1750. But above the centre room of the main range (in which a plaster ceiling had lately to be taken down) an open timber-roof is said to survive as evidence of the earlier date of the erection of the house. Another room contains indeed Late Tudor panelling. – Nice E Gate Lodges with vases in niches.

ZEAL MONACHORUM

ST PETER. W tower with diagonal buttresses at the foot and no pinnacles, S aisle much renewed outside, inside separated from the nave by a granite arcade with A-type piers and capitals only to the main shafts. No N aisle, but a far projecting N transept (the early medieval plan preserved). – FONT. Norman, of tub shape, with little zigzag and cable decoration. – PLATE. Chalice, Paten, Flagon, all by the *Elstons* of Exeter, and all of between 1710 and 1730.

GLOSSARY

ABACUS: flat slab on the top of a capital (q.v.).

ABUTMENT: solid masonry placed to resist the lateral pressure of a vault.

ACANTHUS: plant with thick fleshy and scalloped leaves used as part of the decoration of a Corinthian capital (q.v.) and in some types of leaf carving.

ACHIEVEMENT OF ARMS: in heraldry, a complete display of armorial bearings.

ACROTERION: foliage-carved block on the end or top of a classical pediment.

AEDICULE, AEDICULA: framing of a window or door by columns and a pediment (q.v.).

AMBULATORY: semicircular or polygonal aisle enclosing an apse (q.v.).

ANNULET: *see* Shaft-ring.

ANTIS, IN: *see* Portico.

APSE: vaulted semicircular or polygonal end of a chancel or a chapel.

ARABESQUE: light and fanciful surface decoration using combinations of flowing lines, tendrils, etc., interspersed with vases, animals, etc.

ARCADE: range of arches supported on piers or columns, free-standing; or, BLIND ARCADE, the same attached to a wall.

ARCH: round-headed; i.e. semicircular pointed, i.e. consisting of two curves, each drawn from one centre, and meeting in a point at the top; Segmental,

i.e. in the form of a segment; pointed; four-centred, *see* Fig. 1(*a*); Tudor, *see* Fig. 1(*b*); Ogee, *see* Fig. 1(*c*); Stilted, *see* Fig. 1(*d*).

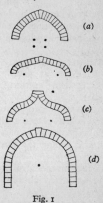

Fig. 1

ARCHITRAVE: lowest of the three main parts of the entablature (q.v.) of an order (q.v.) (*see* Fig. 11).

ARCHIVOLT: undersurface of an arch (also called Soffit).

ARRIS: sharp edge at the meeting of two surfaces.

ASHLAR: masonry of large blocks wrought to even faces and square edges.

ATRIUM: inner court of a Roman house, also open court in front of a church.

ATTACHED: *see* engaged.

ATTIC: topmost storey of a house, if lower than the others.

AUMBREY: recess or cupboard to hold sacred vessels for Mass and Communion.

BAILEY: open space or court of a fortified castle.

BALDACCHINO: canopy supported on columns.

BALLFLOWER: globular flower of three petals enclosing a small ball. A decoration used in the first quarter of the c14.

BALUSTER: small pillar or column of fanciful outline.

BALUSTRADE: series of balusters supporting a handrail or coping (q.v.).

BARBICAN: outwork, constructed like a gateway, defending the entrance to a castle.

BARGEBOARDS: projecting decorated boards placed against the incline of the gable of a building and hiding the horizontal roof timbers.

BASILICA: in medieval architecture an aisled church with a clerestory.

BASTION: projection at the angle of a fortification.

BATTER: wall with an inclined face.

BATTLEMENT: parapet with a series of indentations or embrasures with raised portions or merlons between (also called Crenellation).

BAYS: internal compartments of a building; each divided from the other not by solid walls but by divisions only marked in the side walls (columns, pilasters, etc.) or the ceiling (beams, etc.). Also external divisions of a building by fenestration.

BAY-WINDOW: angular or curved projection of a house front with ample fenestration. If curved also called bow-window; if on an upper floor only also called oriel or oriel window.

BEAKHEAD: Norman ornamental motif consisting of a row of bird or beast heads with beaks pointing downwards and biting usually into a roll moulding.

BELL-COTE: turret usually on the W end of a church to carry the bells.

BILLET: Norman ornamental motif made up of short raised rectangles placed at regular intervals.

BLOCK CAPITAL: Romanesque capital cut from a cube by having the lower angles rounded off to the circular shaft below (also called Cushion Capital) (Fig. 2).

Fig. 2

BOND, ENGLISH or FLEMISH: see Brickwork.

BOSS: knob or projection usually placed to cover the intersection of ribs in a vault.

BOW-WINDOW: see Bay-Window.

BOX PEW: pew with a high wooden enclosure.

BRACES: see Roof.

BRACKET: small supporting piece of stone, etc., to carry a projecting horizontal.

BRICKWORK: Header: brick laid so that the end only appears on the face of the wall. Stretcher: brick laid so that the side only appears on the face of the wall.

English Bond: method of laying bricks so that alternate courses or layers on the face of the wall are composed of headers or stretchers only (Fig. 3*a*).

Flemish Bond: method of laying bricks so that alternate headers and stretchers appear in each course on the face of the wall (Fig. 3*b*).

BROACH: *see* Spire.

BROKEN PEDIMENT: *see* Pediment.

BUTTRESS: mass of brickwork or masonry projecting from or built against a wall to give additional strength. *Angle Buttresses:* two meeting at an angle of 90° at the angle of a building

(*a*)

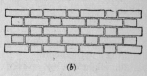

(*b*)

Fig. 3

(Fig. 4*a*). *Diagonal Buttress:* one placed against the right angle formed by two walls, and

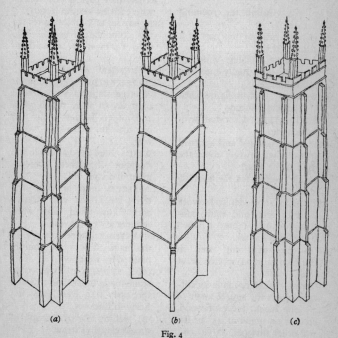

(*a*)   (*b*)   (*c*)

Fig. 4

more or less equiangular with both (Fig. 4*b*). *Flying Buttress:* arch or half arch transmitting the thrust of a vault or roof from the upper part of a wall to an outer support or buttress. *Setback Buttress:* angle buttress set slightly back from the angle (Fig. 4*c*).

CABLE MOULDING: moulding imitating a twisted cord.

CAMBER: slight rise or upward curve of an otherwise horizontal structure.

CAMPANILE: isolated bell tower.

CANOPY: ornamental covering above an altar, pulpit, niche, etc.

CAP: in a windmill the crowning feature.

CAPITAL: head or top part of a column (q.v.).

CARTOUCHE: tablet with an ornate frame, usually enclosing an inscription.

CARYATID: human figure used instead of a column.

CASTELLATED: decorated with battlements.

CEILURE: panelled and adorned part of a wagon-roof above the rood or the altar.

CENSER: vessel for the burning of incense.

CENTERING: wooden framework used in arch and vault construction and removed when the mortar has set.

CHALICE: small cup used in the Communion service or at Mass.

CHAMFER: surface made by cutting across the square angle of a stone block, piece of wood, etc., at an angle of 45° to the two other surfaces.

CHANCEL: that part of the E end of a church in which the altar is placed, usually applied to the whole continuation of the nave E of the crossing.

CHANCEL ARCH: arch at the W end of the chancel.

CHANTRY CHAPEL: chapel attached to, or inside, a church endowed for the saying of Masses for the soul of the founder or some other individual.

CHEVET: French term for the E end of a church (chancel, ambulatory, and radiating chapels).

CHEVRON: sculptured moulding forming a zigzag.

CHOIR: that part of the church where divine service is sung.

CIBORIUM: box or container for the consecrated bread. Also used to mean a baldacchino (q.v.).

CINQUEFOIL: *see* Foil.

CLAPPER BRIDGE: bridge made of large slabs of stone, some built up to make rough piers and other longer ones laid on top to make the roadway.

CLASSIC: here used to mean the moment of highest achievement of a style.

CLASSICAL: here used as the term for Greek and Roman architecture and any subsequent styles copying it.

CLERESTORY: upper storey of the nave walls of a church, pierced by windows.

COADE STONE: artificial (cast) stone made in the late C18 and the early C19 by Coade and Seely in London.

COB: walling material made of mixed clay and straw.

COFFERING: decorating a ceiling with sunk square or polygonal ornamental panels.

COLLAR-BEAM: *see* Roof.

COLONNADE: range of columns.

COLONNETTE: small column.

COLUMNA ROSTRATA: column decorated with carved prows of ships to celebrate a naval victory.

COMPOSITE: *see* Orders.

CONSOLE: bracket (q.v.) with a compound curved outline.

COPING: capping or covering to a wall.

CORBEL: block of stone projecting from a wall, supporting some horizontal feature.

CORBEL TABLE: series of corbels, occurring just below the roof eaves externally or internally, often seen in Norman buildings.

CORINTHIAN: *see* Orders.

CORNICE: in classical architecture the top section of the entablature (q.v.). Also for a projecting decorative feature along the top of a wall, arch, etc.

COVE, COVING: concave undersurface in the nature of a hollow moulding but on a larger scale.

COVER PATEN: cover to a Communion cup, suitable for use as a paten or plate for the consecrated bread.

CRADLE ROOF: *see* Wagon-roof.

CRENELLATION: *see* Battlement.

CREST, CRESTING: ornamental finish along the top of a screen, etc.

CROCKET, CROCKETING: decorative features placed on the sloping sides of spires, pinnacles, gables, etc. in Gothic architecture, carved in various leaf shapes and placed at regular intervals.

CROCKET CAPITAL: *see* Fig. 5.

Fig. 5

CROSSING: space at the intersection of nave, chancel, and transepts.

CRUCK: big curved beam supporting both walls and roof of a cottage.

CRYPT: underground room usually below the E end of a church.

CUPOLA: small polygonal or circular domed turret crowning a roof.

CURTAIN WALL: connecting wall between the towers of a castle.

CURVILINEAR: *see* Tracery.

CUSHION CAPITAL: *see* Block Capital.

CUSP: in tracery (q.v.) the small pointed member between two lobes of a trefoil, quatrefoil, etc.

DADO: decorative covering of the lower part of a wall.

DAGGER: tracery motif of the Dec. style. It is a lancet shape rounded or pointed at the head, pointed at the foot and cusped inside (*see* Fig. 6).

Fig. 6

DAIS: raised platform at one end of a room.

DEC. ('DECORATED'): historical division of English Gothic architecture covering the first half of the C14.

DEMI-COLUMNS: columns half sunk into a wall.

DIAPER WORK: surface decoration composed of square or lozenge shapes.

DOG-TOOTH: typical E.E. ornament consisting of a series of four-cornered stars placed diagonally and raised pyramidally (Fig. 7).

Fig. 7

DOMICAL VAULT: see Vault.

DONJON: see Keep.

DORIC: see Orders.

DORMER (WINDOW): window placed vertically in the sloping plane of a roof.

DRIPSTONE: see Hood-mould.

DRUM: circular or polygonal vertical wall of a dome or cupola.

E.E. ('EARLY ENGLISH'): historical division of English Gothic architecture roughly covering the C13.

EASTER SEPULCHRE: recess with tomb-chest usually in the wall of a chancel, the tomb-chest to receive an effigy of Christ for Easter celebrations.

EAVES: underpart of a sloping roof overhanging a wall.

EAVES CORNICE: cornice below the eaves of a roof.

ECHINUS: quarter round moulding carved with egg and dart pattern, used in classical architecture.

EMBATTLED: see Battlement.

EMBRASURE: small opening in the wall or parapet of a fortified building, usually splayed on the inside. See Loop.

ENCAUSTIC TILES: earthenware glazed and decorated tiles used for paving.

ENGAGED COLUMNS: columns attached to, or partly sunk into, a wall.

ENGLISH BOND: see Brickwork.

ENTABLATURE: in Classical architecture the whole of the horizontal members above a column (that is architrave, frieze, and cornice) (see Fig. 11).

ENTASIS: very slight convex deviation from a straight line; used on Greek columns and sometimes on spires to prevent an optical illusion of concavity.

ENTRESOL: see Mezzanine.

EPITAPH: hanging wall monument.

ESCUTCHEON: shield for armorial bearings.

EXEDRA: the apsidal end of a room. See Apse.

EXTRADOS: outer surface of an arch.

FAIENCE: decorated glazed earthenware.

FAN TRACERY: see Tracery.

FAN VAULT: see Vault.

FERETORY: place behind the High Altar, where the chief shrine of a church is kept.

FESTOON: carved garland of flowers and fruit suspended at both ends.

FILLET: narrow flat band running down a shaft or along a roll moulding.

FINIAL: in Gothic architecture the top of a pinnacle, gable, or bench-end carved into a leaf or leaf-like form.

FLAGON: jug for the wine used in the Communion service.

FLAMBOYANT: properly the latest phase of French Gothic architecture where the window tracery takes on wavy undulating lines.

FLÈCHE: slender wooden spire on the centre of a roof (also called Spirelet).

FLEMISH BOND: see Brickwork.

FLEURON: decorative carved flower or leaf.

FLUTING: vertical channelling in the shaft of a column.

FLYING BUTTRESS: see Buttress.

FOIL: lobe formed by the cusping (q.v.) of a circle or an arch. Trefoil, quatrefoil, cinquefoil, multifoil, express the number of leaf shapes to be seen.

FOLIATED: carved with leaf shapes.

FOSSE: ditch.

FOUR-CENTRED ARCH: see Arch.

FRATER: refectory or dining hall of a monastery.

FRESCO: wall painting on wet plaster.

FRIEZE: middle division of a classical entablature (q.v.) (see Fig. 11).

FRONTAL: covering of the front of an altar.

GALILEE: chapel or vestibule at the w end of a church enclosing the porch. Also called Narthex (q.v.).

GALLERY: in church architecture upper storey above an aisle, opened in arches to the nave. Also called Tribune (q.v.) and often erroneously Triforium (q.v.).

GARGOYLE: water spout projecting from the parapet of a wall or tower; carved into a human or animal shape.

GAZEBO: lookout tower or raised summer house in a picturesque garden.

'GEOMETRICAL': see Tracery.

'GIBBS' SURROUND: of a doorway or window. A surround with alternating larger and smaller blocks of stone, quoinwise, or intermittent large blocks, sometimes with a narrow raised band connecting them up the verticals and along the extrados of the arch (Fig. 8).

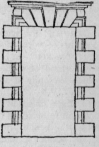

Fig. 8

GROIN: sharp edge at the meeting of two cells of a cross-vault.

GROINED VAULT: see Vault.

GROTESQUE: fanciful ornamental decoration: see Arabesque.

HAGIOSCOPE: see Squir

HALF-TIMBERING: see Framing.

HALL CHURCH: church in nave and aisles are of height or approximately s

HAMMER-BEAM: see Roof.

HANAP: large metal cup, generally made for domestic use, standing on an elaborate base and stem; with a very ornate cover frequently crowned with a little steeple.

HEADERS: see Brickwork.

HERRINGBONE WORK: brick, stone, or tile construction where the component blocks are laid diagonally instead of flat. Alternate courses lie in opposing directions to make a zigzag pattern up the face of the wall.

HIPPED ROOF: see Roof.

HOOD-MOULD: projecting moulding above an arch or a lintel to throw off water (also called Dripstone or Label).

ICONOGRAPHY: the science of the contents of works of art.

IMPOST: brackets in walls, usually formed of mouldings, on which the ends of an arch rest.

INDENT: shape chiselled out in a stone slab to receive a brass.

INGLENOOK: bench or seat built in beside a fireplace, sometimes covered by the chimney breast, occasionally lit by small windows on each side of the fire.

INTERCOLUMNATION: the space between columns.

IONIC: see Orders (Fig. 11).

JAMB: straight side of an archway, doorway, or window.

KEEL MOULDING: moulding whose outline is in section like that of the keel of a ship.

KEEP: massive tower of a Norman castle.

KEYSTONE: middle stone in an arch.

KING-POST: see Roof (Fig. 13).

LABEL: see Hood-mould.

LABEL STOP: ornamental boss at the end of a hood-mould (q.v.).

LANCET WINDOW: slender pointed-arched window.

LANTERN: in architecture, a small circular or polygonal turret with windows all round crowning a roof (see Cupola) or a dome.

LANTERN CROSS: churchyard cross with lantern-shaped top usually with sculptured representations on the sides of the top.

LEAN-TO ROOF: roof with one slope only, built against a higher wall.

LESENE or PILASTER STRIP: pilaster without base and capital.

LIERNE: see Vault (Fig. 20).

LINENFOLD: Tudor panelling ornamented with a conventional representation of a piece of linen laid in vertical folds. The piece is repeated in each panel.

LINTEL: horizontal beam or stone bridging an opening.

LOGGIA: recessed colonnade (q.v.).

LONG AND SHORT WORK: Saxon quoins (q.v.) consisting of stones placed with the long sides alternately upright and horizontal.

LOUVRE: opening, often with lantern (q.v.) over, in the roof of a room to let the smoke from a central hearth escape.

LOZENGE: diamond shape.

LUNETTE: tympanum (q.v.) or curved opening in a vault.

LYCH GATE: wooden gate structure with a roof and open sides placed at the entrance to a churchyard to provide space for the reception of a coffin. The word lych is Saxon and means a corpse.

MACHICOLATION: projecting gallery on brackets constructed on the outside of castle towers or walls. The gallery has holes in the floor to drop missiles through.

MAJOLICA: ornamented glazed earthenware.

MANSARD: see Roof.

MERLON: see Battlement.

METOPE: in classical architecture of the Doric order (q.v.) the space in the frieze between the triglyphs (Fig. 11).

MEZZANINE: low storey placed between two higher ones.

MISERERE: see Misericord.

MISERICORD: bracket placed on the underside of a hinged choir stall seat which, when turned up, provided the occupant of the seat with a support during long periods of standing (also called Miserere).

MODILLION: small bracket of which large numbers (modillion frieze) are often placed below a cornice (q.v.) in classical architecture.

MOTTE: steep mound forming the main feature of C11 and C12 castles.

MOUCHETTE: tracery motif in

Fig. 9

curvilinear tracery, a curved dagger (q.v.) (Fig. 9).

MULLION: vertical post or upright dividing a window into two or more 'lights'.

NAILHEAD: E.E. ornamental motif, consisting of small pyramids regularly repeated (Fig. 10).

Fig. 10

NARTHEX: enclosed vestibule or covered porch at the main entrance to a church (see Galilee).

NEWEL: central post in a circular or winding staircase; also the principal post when a flight of stairs meets a landing.

OBELISK: lofty pillar of square section tapering at the top and ending pyramidally.

OGEE: see Arch (Fig. 1c).

ORATORY: small private chapel in a house.

ORDER: (1) of a doorway or window: series of concentric steps receding towards the opening; (2) in classical architecture: column with base, shaft, capital, and entablature (q.v.) according to one of the following styles: Greek Doric, Roman Doric, Tuscan Doric, Ionic, Corinthian, Composite. The established details are very elaborate, and some specialist architectural work should be consulted for further guidance (see Fig. 11).

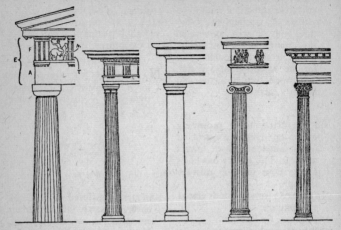

Fig. 11 – Orders of Columns (Greek Doric, Roman Doric, Tuscan, Ionic, Corinthian)
E, Entablature; F, Frieze; A, Architrave; M, Metope; T. Triglyph

ORIEL: *see* Bay Window.

OVERHANG: projection of the upper storey of a house.

OVERSAILING COURSES: series of stone or brick courses, each one projecting beyond the one below it.

PALIMPSEST: (1) *of a brass:* where a metal plate has been re-used by turning over and engraving on the back; (2) *of a wall painting:* where one overlaps and partly obscures an earlier one.

PALLADIAN: architecture following the ideas and principles of Andrea Palladio, 1518–80.

PANTILE: tile of curved S-shaped section.

PARAPET: low wall placed to protect any spot where there is a sudden drop, for example on a bridge, quay, hillside, house-top, etc.

PARGETTING: plaster work with patterns and ornaments either in relief or engraved on it.

PARVISE: room over a church porch. Often used as a school-house or a store room.

PATEN: plate to hold the bread at Communion or Mass.

PATERA: small flat circular or oval ornament in classical architecture.

PEDIMENT: low-pitched gable (q.v.) used in classical, Renaissance, and neo-classical architecture above a portico and above doors, windows, etc. It may be straight-sided or curved segmentally. *Open Pediment:* one where the centre portion of the base is left open. *Broken Pediment:* one where the centre portion of the sloping sides is 'broken' out.

PENDANT: boss (q.v.) elongated so that it seems to hang down.

PENDENTIF: concave triangular spandrel used to lead from the angle of two walls to the base of a circular dome. It is constructed as part of the hemisphere over a diameter the size of the diagonal of the basic square (Fig. 12).

Fig. 12

PERP (PERPENDICULAR): historical division of English Gothic architecture roughly covering the period from 1350 to 1530.

PIANO NOBILE: principal storey of a house with the reception rooms; usually the first floor.

PIAZZA: square open space surrounded by buildings, in C17 and C18 English sometimes used to mean a long colonnade or loggia.

PIER: strong, solid support, frequently square in section or of composite section (compound pier).

PIETRA DURA: ornamental or scenic inlay by means of thin slabs of stone.

PILASTER: shallow pier attached to a wall.

PILLAR PISCINA: free-standing piscina on a pillar.

PINNACLE: ornamental form crowning a spire, tower, buttress, etc., usually of steep pyramidal, conical, or some similar shape.

PISCINA: basin for washing the Communion or Mass vessels, provided with a drain. Generally set in or against the wall to the S of an altar.

PLAISANCE: summer-house, pleasure house near a mansion.

PLATE TRACERY: see Tracery.

PLINTH: projecting base of a wall or column, generally chamfered (q.v.) or moulded at the top.

POPPYHEAD: ornament of leaf and flower type used to decorate the tops of bench or stall-ends.

PORTCULLIS: gate constructed to rise and fall in vertical grooves; used in gateways of castles.

PORTE COCHERE: porch large enough to admit wheeled vehicles.

PORTICO: centre-piece of a house or a church with classical detached or attached columns and a pediment. A portico is called *prostyle* or *in antis* according to whether it projects from or recedes into a building. In a portico *in antis* the columns range with the side walls.

POSTERN: small gateway at the back of a building.

PREDELLA: in an altar-piece the horizontal strip below the main representation, often used for a number of subsidiary representations in a row

PRESBYTERY: the part of the church lying E of the choir. It is the part where altar is placed.

PRINCIPAL: *see* Roof (Fig. 13).

PRIORY: monastic house whose head is a prior or prioress, not an abbot or abbess.

PROSTYLE: with free-standing columns in a row.

PULPITUM: stone rood screen in a major church.

PURLIN: *see* Roof (Figs. 13, 14).

PUTTO: small naked boy.

QUADRANGLE: inner courtyard in a large building complex.

QUARRY: in stained-glass work, a small diamond or square-shaped piece of glass set diagonally.

QUATREFOIL: *see* Foil.

QUEEN-POSTS: *see* Roof (Fig. 14).

QUOINS: dressed stones at the angles of a building. Sometimes all the stones are of the same size; more often they are alternately large or small.

RADIATING CHAPELS: chapels projecting radially from an ambulatory or an apse.

RAFTER: *see* Roof.

RAMPART: stone wall, or wall of earth surrounding a castle, fortress, or fortified city.

RAMPART-WALK: path along the inner face of a rampart.

REBATE: channel or small recess cut into a piece of wood or stone longitudinally to receive the edge of some member that is to be secured in it. The depth of the channel is equal to the thickness of the member to be let into it.

REBUS: pun, a play on words. The literal translation and illustration of a name for artistic and heraldic purposes (Belton=bell, tun).

REEDING: decoration with parallel convex mouldings touching one another.

REFECTORY: Dining hall; *see* Frater.

RENDERING: plastering of an outer wall.

REPOUSSÉ: decoration of metal work by relief designs, formed by beating the metal from the back.

REREDOS: structure behind and above an altar.

RESPOND: half-pier bonded into a wall and carrying one end of an arch.

RETABLE: altar-piece, a picture or piece of carving, standing behind and attached to an altar.

RETICULATION: *see* Tracery (Fig. 19).

REVEAL: that part of a jamb (q.v.) which lies between the glass or door and the outer surface of the wall.

RIB VAULT: *see* Vault.

ROCOCO: latest phase of the Baroque style, current in most Continental countries between *c.* 1720 and *c.* 1760.

ROMANESQUE: that style in architecture which was current in the C11 and C12 and preceded the Gothic style (in England often called Norman).

ROOD: cross or crucifix.

ROOD LOFT: singing gallery on the top of the rood screen, often supported by a coving.

ROOD SCREEN: *see* Screen.

ROOD STAIRS: stairs to give access to the rood loft.

ROOF: *Hipped:* roof with sloped instead of vertical ends. *Mansard:* roof with a double slope, the lower slope being larger and steeper than the upper. *Saddleback:* tower roof shaped like an ordinary gabled timber roof. The following members have special names: *Rafter:* roof-timber sloping up from the wall plate to the ridge. *Principal:* principal rafter, usually corresponding to the main bay divisions of the nave or chancel below. *Wall Plate:* timber laid longitudinally on the top of a wall. *Purlin:* longitudinal member laid parallel with wall plate and ridge beam some way up the slope of the roof. *Tie-beam:* beam connecting the two slopes of a roof across at its foot, usually at the height of the wall plate, to prevent the roof from spreading. *Collar-beam:* tie-beam applied higher up the slope of the roof. *Strut:* upright timber connecting the tie-beam with the rafter above it. *King-post:*

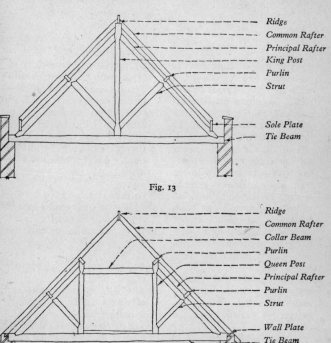

Ridge
Common Rafter
Principal Rafter
King Post
Purlin
Strut
Sole Plate
Tie Beam

Fig. 13

Ridge
Common Rafter
Collar Beam
Purlin
Queen Post
Principal Rafter
Purlin
Strut
Wall Plate
Tie Beam

Fig. 14

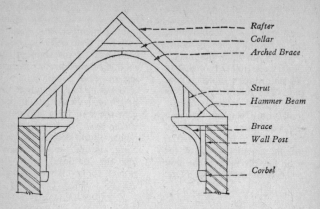

Fig. 15

upright timber connecting a tie-beam and collar-beam with the ridge-beam. *Queen-posts:* two struts placed symmetrically on a tie-beam or collar-beam. *Braces:* inclined timbers inserted to strengthen others. Usually braces connect a collar-beam with the rafters below or a tie-beam with the wall below. Braces can be straight or curved (also called arched). *Hammer-beam:* beam projecting at right angles, usually from the top of a wall, to carry arched braces or struts and arched braces (*see* Figs. 13, 14, 15).

ROSE WINDOW (or WHEEL WINDOW): circular window with patterned tracery arranged to radiate from the centre.

ROTUNDA: building circular in plan.

RUBBLE: building stones, not square or hewn, nor laid in regular courses.

RUSTICATION: Ashlar-work of blocks with the margins only wrought and the faces rough or specially rock-faced: or ashlar-work of smooth-faced blocks with the joints greatly emphasized (smooth rustication). If only the horizontal joints are emphasized it is called banded rustication.

SADDLEBACK: *see* Roof.

SALTIRE CROSS: equal-limbed cross placed diagonally.

SANCTUARY: area around the main altar of a church (*see* Presbytery).

SARCOPHAGUS: elaborately carved coffin.

SCAGLIOLA: material composed of cement and colouring matter to imitate marble.

SCALLOPED CAPITAL: development of the block capital (q.v.) in which the single semi-circular surface is elaborated into a series of truncated cones (Fig. 16).

Fig. 16

SCARP: artificial cutting away of the ground to form a steep slope.

SCREEN: *Parclose screen:* screen separating a chapel from the rest of a church. *Rood screen:* screen at the W end of a chancel. Above it on the rood-beam was the rood (q.v.).

SCREENS PASSAGE: passage between the entrances to kitchen, buttery, etc., and the screen behind which lies the hall of a medieval house.

SEDILIA: seats for the priests (usually three) on the S side of the chancel of a church.

SEGMENTAL ARCH: *see* Arch.

SET-OFF: *see* Weathering.

SEXPARTITE: *see* Vaulting.

SGRAFFITO: pattern incised into plaster so as to expose a dark surface underneath.

SHAFT-RING: ring round a circular pier or a shaft attached to a pier.

SILL: lower horizontal part of the frame of a window.

SLATEHANGING: the covering of walls by overlapping rows of slates, on a timber substructure.

SOFFIT: *see* Archivolt.

SOLAR: upper drawing-room of a medieval house.

SOPRAPORTE: painting above the door of a room, usual in the C17 and C18.

SOUNDING BOARD: horizontal board or canopy over a pulpit. Also called Tester.

SPANDREL: triangular surface between one side of an arch, the horizontal drawn from its apex, and the vertical drawn from its springer, also the surface between two arches.

SPIRE: tall pyramidal or conical pointed erection often built on top of a tower, turret, etc. *Broach Spire:* spire which is generally octagonal in plan rising from the top or parapet of a square tower. A small inclined piece of masonry covers the vacant triangular space at each of the four angles of the square and is carried up to a point along the diagonal sides of the octagon. *Needle Spire:* thin spire rising from the centre of a tower roof, well inside the parapet.

SPIRELET: *see* Flèche.

SPLAY: chamfer, usually of the jamb of a window.

SPRINGING: level at which an arch rises from its supports.

SQUINCH: arch or system of concentric arches thrown across the angle between two walls to support a superstructure, for example a dome (Fig. 17).

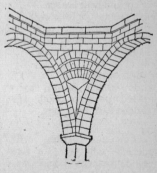

Fig. 17

SQUINT: hole cut in a wall or through a pier to allow a view of the main altar of a church from places whence it could not otherwise be seen (also called Hagioscope).

STALL: carved seat, one in a row, made of wood or stone.

STEEPLE: the tower or spire of a church.

STIFF-LEAF: E.E. type of foliage of many-lobed shapes (Fig. 18).

STILTED: *see* Arch.

Fig. 18

STOUP: vessel for the reception of holy water, usually placed near a door.

STRAINER ARCH: arch inserted across a room to prevent the walls from leaning.

STRAPWORK: C16 decoration consisting of interlaced bands, and forms similar to fretwork or cut and bent leather.

STRETCHERS: *see* Brickwork.

STRING COURSE: projecting horizontal band or moulding set in the surface of a wall.

STRUT: *see* Roof.

STUCCO: plaster work.

SWAG: festoon formed by a carved piece of cloth suspended from both ends.

TABERNACLE: richly ornamented niche (q.v.) or freestanding canopy. Usually contains the Holy Sacrament.

TAZZA: shallow bowl on a foot.

TERMINAL FIGURES (TERMS, TERMINI): upper part of a human figure growing out of a pier, pilaster, etc., which tapers towards the base.

TERRACOTTA: burnt clay, unglazed.

TESSELATED PAVEMENT: decorative floor or wall covering made up of tesserae or small coloured cubes of stone, fitted into a bed of cement.

TESTER: *see* Sounding Board.

THREE-DECKER PULPIT: pulpit with Clerk's Stall and Reading Desk placed below each other.

TIE-BEAM: *see* Roof (Figs. 13, 14).

TIERCERON: *see* Vault (Fig. 20).

TILEHANGING: *see* Slatehanging.

TIMBER-FRAMING: method of construction where walls are built of timber framework with the spaces filled in by plaster or brickwork. Sometimes the timber is covered over with plaster or boarding laid horizontally.

TOMB-CHEST: chest-shaped stone coffin, the most usual medieval form of funeral monument.

TOUCH: soft black marble quarried near Tournai.

TOURELLE: turret corbelled out from the wall.

TRACERY: intersecting ribwork in the upper part of a window, or used decoratively in blank arches, on vaults, etc. *Plate tracery:* early form of tracery where decoratively shaped openings are cut through the solid stone infilling in the head of a window. *Bar tracery:* intersecting ribwork made up of slender shafts, continuing the lines of the mullions of windows up to a decorative mesh in the head of the window. *Geometrical tracery:* tracery consisting chiefly of circles or foiled circles. *Intersected tracery:* tracery in which each mullion of a window branches out into two curved bars in such a way that every one of them runs concentrically with the others against the arch of the whole window. The result is that every light of the window is a lancet and every two, three, four, etc., lights together form a pointed arch. *Reticulated tracery:* tracery consisting entirely of circles drawn at top and bottom into ogee shapes so that a net-like appearance results (Fig. 19).

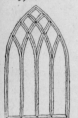

Fig. 19

TRANSEPT: transverse portion of a cross-shaped church.

TRANSOME: horizontal bar across the opening of a window.

TRANSVERSE ARCH: *see* Vaulting.

TRIBUNE: *see* Gallery.

TRICIPUT, SIGNUM TRICIPUT: sign of the Trinity expressed by three faces belonging to one head.

TRIFORIUM: arcaded wall passage or blank arcading facing the nave at the height of the aisle roof and below the clerestory (q.v.) windows. (*See* Gallery.)

TRIGLYPHS: blocks with vertical grooves separating the metopes (q.v.) in the Doric frieze (Fig. 11).

TROPHY: sculptured group of arms or armour, used as a memorial of victory.

TRUMEAU: stone mullion (q.v.) supporting the tympanum (q.v.) of a wide doorway.

TURRET: very small tower, round or polygonal in plan.

TUSCAN: *see* Order.

TYMPANUM: space between the lintel of a doorway and the arch above it.

UNDERCROFT: vaulted room, sometimes underground, below a church or chapel.

VAULT: *Barrel vault: see* Tunnel vault. *Cross-vault: see* Groined vault. *Domical vault:* square or polygonal dome rising direct on a square or polygonal bay, the curved surfaces separated by groins (q.v.). *Fan vault:* vault where all ribs springing from one springer are of the same length, the same distance from the next, and the same curvature. *Groined vault* or *Cross-vault:* vault of two tunnel vaults of identical shape intersecting each other at right angles. *Lierne:* tertiary rib, that is, rib which does not spring either from one of the main springers or the central boss. *Quadripartite vault:* one wherein one bay of vaulting is divided into four parts. *Rib vault:* vault with diagonal ribs projecting along the groins. *Ridge-rib:* rib along the longitudinal or transverse ridge of a vault. *Sexpartite vault:* one wherein one bay of quadripartite vaulting is divided into two parts transversely so that each bay of vaulting has six parts. *Tierceron:* secondary rib, that is, rib which issues from one of the main springers or the central boss and leads to a place on a ridge-rib. *Transverse arch:* arch separating one bay of a vault from the next. *Tunnel vault* or *Barrel vault:* vault of semicircular or pointed section (Fig. 20).

VAULTING SHAFT: vertical member leading to the springer of a vault.

VENETIAN WINDOW: window with three openings, the central one arched and wider than the outside ones.

VERANDAH: open gallery or balcony with a roof on light, usually metal, supports.

VESTIBULE: ante-room or entrance hall.

VILLA: according to Gwilt (1842) 'a country house for the residence of opulent persons'.

VITRIFIED: made similar to glass.

VOLUTE: spiral scroll, one of the component parts of an Ionic column (*see* Orders).

VOUSSOIR: wedge-shaped stone used in arch construction.

Wagon-roof: roof in which by closely set rafters with arched braces the appearance

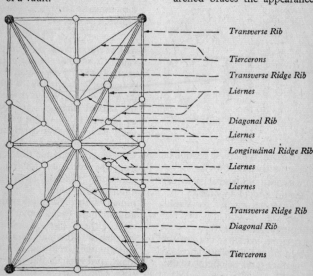

Transverse Rib

Tiercerons

Transverse Ridge Rib

Liernes

Diagonal Rib

Liernes

Longitudinal Ridge Rib

Liernes

Liernes

Transverse Ridge Rib

Diagonal Rib

Tiercerons

Fig. 20

of the inside of a canvas tilt
over a wagon is achieved.
Wagon-roofs can be panelled
or plastered (ceiled) or left
uncovered.

WAINSCOT: timber lining to
walls.

WALL PLATE: *see* Roof.

WATERLEAF: leaf shape used in
later C12 capitals. The waterleaf is a broad, unribbed,
tapering leaf curving up towards the angle of the abacus
and turned in at the top (Fig.
21).

WEATHER-BOARDING: overlapping horizontal boards, covering a timber-framed wall.

Fig. 21

WEATHERING: sloping hori-
zontal surface on sills, buttresses, etc., to throw off water.

WEEPERS: small figures placed
in niches along the sides of some
medieval tombs (also called
Mourners).

WHEEL WINDOW: *see* Rose
Window.

INDEX OF PLATES

INDEX OF ARTISTS

INDEX OF PLACES

*The references in brackets indicate the square in which the
place will be found on the map at the
end of the book*

T O L   C H A N N E

Ilfracombe
Lee   Watermouth
    Cas.
Berrynarbor   Combe
    Martin

Trentishoe
Martinhoe
Lynton
Lynmouth   Countisbury

Georgeham   W. Down   Kentisbury
aunton   Bittadon
unton   Ash Barton   E. Down   Arlington
ardon   Marwood   Loxhore

Brendon
Parracombe

Ashford   Youlston   Shirwell
    Upcott   Goodleigh
remington   Pilton   Bratton
nstow   Barnstaple   Fleming
apley Park   Acland   Stoke
stleigh   Barton   Rivers
    Landkey

E X M O O R

Highbray
Charles

Tawstock   Bishop's
Horwood   Tawton
   Newton   W.
   Tracey   Buckland
Alverdiscott   Swimbridge   Buckland
Huntshaw   Hall   Filleigh   Castle
Yarnscombe   Umberleigh   Hill
  Way   Atherington   Chittlehampton
  Barton
Stevenstone Ho.   Warkleigh
St Giles in the Wood   Satterleigh   South
erly Ho.   High   Molton
   Bickington   George
nscott   Combe Barton   Nympton
Woodleigh   Roborough   King's   Chittlehamholt
ford   Barton   Nympton
eanton   Burrington   Romansleigh
atchville   Ashreigney
  Dolton   Colleton
  Dowland   Barton
Meeth   Rashleigh   Chulmleigh
igh   Barton   Cheldon
Ho.   Chawleigh
Monk   Eggesford   Affeton
kehampton   Winkleigh   Barton
Broadwoodkelly   Brushford   Nymet
    Wembworthy   Rowland

North
Molton
   Twitchen
Whitechapel Barton
    Molland
    West Anstey
Bishops   East Anstey
Nympton
Mariansleigh
  Rose   Knowstone
  Ash
Meshaw
   Rackenford   Oakford
    Stoodleigh
W. Worlington
E. Worlington
Thelbridge   Witheridge   Loxbeare
   Washford Pyne   Washfield
Wonham   Cruwys Morchard   Calverleigh
Puddington   Witheigh   Knights
Morchard   Court
Bishop   Woolfardisworthy
   Poughill   Ag

Exbourne   Coldridge   Lapford
  Honeychurch   Bondleigh   Bury
we   Monachorum   Zeal   Barton
Sompford   N. Tawton   Down
Courtenay   St Mary
Cottles
Barton   Copplestone

Kennerleigh   Stockleigh English
Dowrich   Cheriton   Cadeleigh
Ho.   Fitzpaine
  Upton
  Helions
Sandford

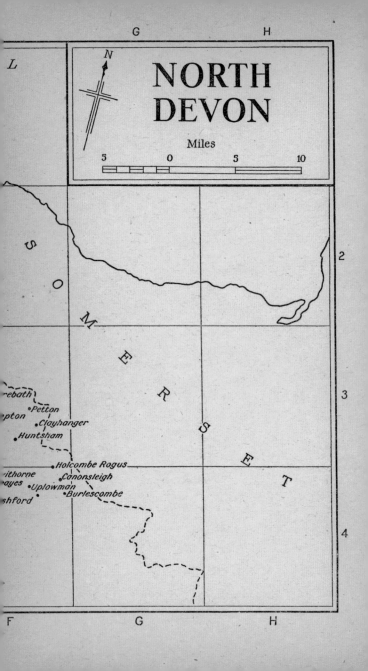

G   H

L

NORTH
DEVON

Miles

5   0   5   10

2

S
O
M
E
R
S
E
T

3

rebath
•Petton
pton •Clayhanger
• Huntsham

•Holcombe Rogus
ithorne •Cononsleigh
ayes •Uplowman
shford• •Burlescombe

4

F   G   H

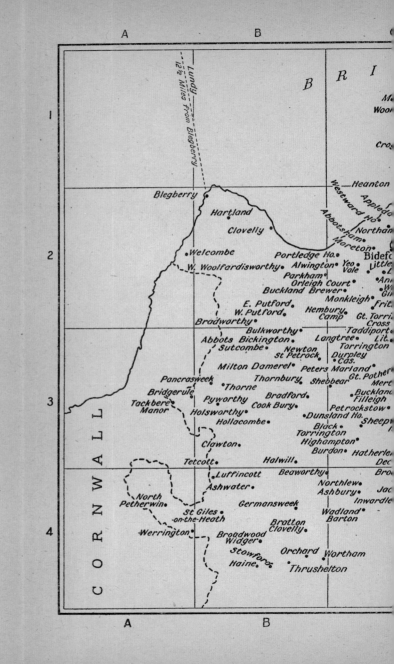

THE BUILDINGS OF
· ENGLAND

'The principle on which these guides to the architecture of all England are being compiled is critical. It is not one of quaintness, oldness or association, the three dictatorial qualities of our guidebook trade. Art is art, excellence is excellence and the counties are being combed for all that is architecturally notable. ... A survey as complete and first-hand as possible, clear arrangement, sixty-four pages of illustrations, and a small price – important, but less so than the rare application to our local buildings of a European scholarship.' – Geoffrey Grigson in *The Observer*

'Inventories these books are, and wonderfully detailed ones. ... But they are much more than that. On every page one is continually made aware – sometimes by a sentence of comment, sometimes by as little as a single word, sometimes even by what isn't said – of learning, intelligence and taste of work, placing, testing, and assessing. So far as architecture is concerned, this series will relegate most other guides to the status of picture books.' – *The Architects' Journal*

'Here is something new and, in its way, as provocative and personal as the most dyed-in-the-soil, know-every-inch-of-it county book can be.' – John Summerson in *The New Statesman and Nation*

'He has a sharp eye for the small things that the guidebook writer who follows orthodox paths invariably misses, and the knowledge to label them accurately. They are a masterly work of condensation.' – J. M. Richards in *The Listener*

Other volumes now available are *Cornwall, Nottinghamshire, Middlesex* (3s 6d each) and *London (except the Cities of London and Westminster)* (6s). *South Devon* will follow shortly.